picture books

an annotated bibliography with activities for teaching writing with the 6+1 Trait® Writing model

Sixth Edition, 2004

Peter Bellamy, Editor

NWREL

Northwest Regional Educational Laboratory

Portland, Oregon

Northwest Regional Educational Laboratory
101 SW Main Street, Suite 500
Portland, Oregon 97204
(503) 275-9500
www.nwrel.org

Center for Research, Evaluation, and Assessment
Dr. Kim Yap, Senior Program Director
Assessment Program
Dr. Michael Kozlow, Program Director

ISBN 0-89354-026-9

Contents

Preface

If this is your first connection with our picture book bibliography, welcome. If you purchased this sixth edition to get the latest, most up-to-date copy, then you are in for a treat. We have been busy reading and reviewing many picture books this year, and it is with great pleasure that we recommend these titles to you. You will notice that the traits have been expanded to include Presentation for the first time. We are certain that you will find something here to fit every taste and occasion, no matter the grade level you teach, your subject area, or your interests.

This edition adds many new books published between 1998 and 2004, and suggests a link for each to one of the traits of the 6+1 Trait® Writing model. But don't limit yourself to just one trait for each book, because many encompass more, if not all, of the traits. Use the books as an inspiration to you and your student writers in whatever ways suit your plans and your curriculum. This edition contains lessons to use as they are, or to expand and elaborate. If you come up with a brilliant new strategy for using one of the books, let us know so we can share it in a future *Picture Books* and give you credit for your work.

The first section of the collection is arranged alphabetically within the 6+1 Trait® Writing model: Ideas, Organization, Voice, Word Choice, Sentence Fluency, Conventions, and Presentation. The second section of the book, the collection of teaching activities, is also organized by trait.

This publication is growing; there are almost 150 new titles in this edition. We have maintained the author and title index guides at the back to make your searching task a little easier. We have also added a coding for Young Adult books suitable for use with older listeners (YA). Use these indices to find new and familiar authors, titles, and classroom lessons for all ages.

This new and expanded edition results from the efforts of many, notably Sharon Northern, who worked tirelessly to bring together the pieces of this and prior editions. Also noteworthy are the earlier efforts of Ruth Culham and Vicki Spandel, visionaries and advocates for the effectiveness of trait-based writing assessment, whose original work culminated in preceding *Picture Books* editions, upon which this new edition builds.

We hope that you find this expanded *Picture Books* edition a valuable reference and resource in your teaching role.

For more information about training opportunities and additional support materials, including our videotape *Picture This: Using Picture Books With Middle and High School Writers,* please contact us at 1-800-547-6339. There is an order form in the back of the book for those who wish to order 6+1 Trait® materials.

Introduction

The traits referred to in *Picture Books* come from the combined wisdom of thousands and thousands of teachers and more than 15 years of careful research and analysis of student work. We call it simply 6+1 Trait® Writing because time and time again, these same characteristics show up on teachers', parents', students', and community members' lists of what makes effective writing. They are:

Ideas—The heart of the message, the content of the piece, the main theme, together with the details that enrich and develop that theme.

Organization—The internal structure of the piece, the thread of central meaning, the logical and sometimes intriguing pattern of ideas.

Voice—The heart and soul, the magic, and the wit, along with the feelings and conviction of the individual writer coming out through the words.

Word Choice—The use of rich, colorful, precise language that moves and enlightens the reader.

Sentence Fluency—The rhythm and flow of the language, the sound of word patterns, the way in which the writing plays to the ear, not just to the eye.

Conventions—The mechanical correctness of the piece: spelling, grammar and usage, paragraphing, capitals, and punctuation.

Presentation—The form and appearance of the text that enhances the ability of the reader to understand and connect with the message.

These traits are the foundation of a shared language that enables teachers and students to talk and work together as writers. It is possible to consider the effect of all seven traits on a piece of writing, or to look at one trait at a time. And, the exciting part is that these criteria, this shared vocabulary, can be explained and taught to students of all ages so they become their own best partner in the revising and editing process. When students really understand what makes writing—any kind of writing—work effectively, they can take ownership of the writing process. They learn from the criteria and internalize them so that the language of the traits becomes a powerful revision tool.

This approach to assessment is highly flexible and a natural entry into thoughtful decisionmaking relating to quality instruction. Using the scoring guide as an instructional tool provides the vital link between assessment and instruction. At last we can describe clearly for students exactly what we mean by quality work.

Picture Books is only one resource available to help teachers link writing assessment and instruction. We hope you'll find it useful and motivating.

Annotated Bibliography

The following pages contain an alphabetized collection of annotated picture book titles organized by trait. But by no means should you assume that there is only one possibility for using these books as resources in your classroom. In fact, each book has limitless possibilities!

For example, here's an idea suggested by several school districts that have successfully used previous editions of the *Picture Books* bibliography as a resource for teaching writing. Media specialists or district language arts specialists purchase a dozen or more books from each of the recommended lists for each trait. They package each of these smaller collections in boxes or containers as kits, label them by trait, and have these kits available to loan to classroom teachers in their schools or across districts.

Here are some other ideas:

- Use the kits as they are, then ask teachers to include the names of books they'd like to see added before they borrow it again. This way, the kits grow to reflect titles and topics important to local issues and curriculum.

- Select enough titles from *Picture Books* (from your local library/media center and classroom) so that each child has three or four to read. Ask students to read their books and have them stack each one in piles labeled Ideas, Organization, Voice, Word Choice, Sentence Fluency, Conventions, and Presentation. Compare their choices with those in the bibliography.

- Develop a lesson to go with one or more of the books from the bibliography. Put a copy of that lesson in the kit of books on that trait when you return it. Who knows? Maybe when you check out the set of books next year, there will be lots of new lessons tucked in for you to copy. (Just think of the possibilities!)

One more thing before you turn the page and begin to enjoy the list of wonderful picture books just waiting for you ... this list is NOT complete. These book titles are only the ones we have been fortunate enough to find. You probably have many more titles at your fingertips that will work just as well for teaching the seven traits of writing—old favorites and new. Please consider this as a starter kit of titles and ideas and take it from here.

Ideas

Clarity and focus
Rich and vivid details
A clear sense of purpose

Adler, David. *Mama Played Baseball.* Gulliver Books, 2003. Hardcover: ISBN 0-15-202196-5. This book captures the essence of the short-lived All American Girls Professional Baseball League formed in 1943 and disbanded in 1954. With war raging in Europe and the Pacific, many players for men's leagues enlisted in the military. The women's league was created to fill the need for the national sport to continue for those still at home. This story reflects the view of a youngster seeing her mother in the uniform of a professional baseball player, while her father wears the uniform of a soldier. Illustrations by Chris O'Leary effectively capture the atmosphere of the time. (YA)

Allard, Harry. *Miss Nelson Is Back.* Houghton Mifflin, 1982. Hardcover: ISBN 0-395-32956-6. Do your students experiment by adding elements of suspense to their stories? See if they can imitate the style of this charming story in their own work. Students could also try their hand at turning Miss Nelson into other delightful characters and learn a little more about character development. What if they had the opportunity to rewrite this story using one of their current teachers?

Allen, Debbie. *Dancing in the Wings.* Dial Books, 2000. Hardcover (LB)*: ISBN 0-8037-2501-9. Based on her own experience, this story by dancer/actress/producer Debbie Allen is one to inspire determination. Everyone says that Sassy is too tall and her feet too big to be a ballet dancer. But a tryout to go to an important dance festival changes everyone's opinion, as well as Sassy's life. The humor of the story is matched by colorful illustrations. Also good for the trait of word choice.

Angelou, Maya. *Kofi and His Magic.* Clarkson Potter, 1996. Hardcover: ISBN 0-517-70453-6. Maya Angelou … you have to know that this is a book of beauty and wonder. A young West African boy, Kofi, from a town known for its beautifully woven Kente cloth, tells a magical story of imagination that allows us all to journey to neighboring towns, meet different people, and experience life all over his country. With the warp and the weft of his town's cloth to deftly weave the story together, this piece is bound to teach and delight. (Featured in the *Seeing With New Eyes* video.)

* (LB) signifies library binding.

Arnold, Ann. *The Adventurous Chef: Alexis Soyer.* Frances Foster Books, 2002. Hardcover: ISBN 0-374-31665-1.

Born in France, Alexis Soyer traveled to England where he hoped to make his fortune as a chef cooking for the rich and famous of the British aristocracy. But no sooner had he established himself and his reputation than he became embroiled in concern over the appalling conditions for soldiers fighting in the Crimea. Soyer determined to use his skills as a chef to improve the food of the British Army. He joined nurse Florence Nightingale, and together they revolutionized both the medical treatment given to wounded and sick soldiers, and the quality of the army's cooking and meals. A fascinating rendition of a little-known true story. (YA)

Bash, Barbara. *Tree of Life: The World of the African Baobab.* Sierra Club Books (Little, Brown), 2002. Paperback: ISBN 1-578-05086-3.

In graceful calligraphic text rich with detail, Bash tells the fascinating life cycle story of the African tree of life. Magnificent watercolor illustrations complement the text, showing the baobab as a nesting site for the yellow-collared lovebird and other colorful, bright-feathered inhabitants; a home for tiny sweat bees and numerous other insects; a twilight shelter for the timid and elflike bush babies; a shady hideout for impalas; and a hearty meal for bark-loving elephants. Discover, through text that informs and entertains at the same time, a dozen other roles this tree plays in the fabric of African life. An excellent illustration of how to select just the right details and how to recount them in a way that involves and enlightens readers.

Baylor, Byrd. *Everybody Needs a Rock.* Bt Bound, 1999. Hardcover (LB): ISBN 0-808-59418-4.

Think rocks all look pretty much alike? Byrd Baylor's lyrical book teaches readers to look for that special rock that is theirs alone, and to notice and appreciate its specialness. Read this one, then have students search for and write about their own rocks. (YA)

Baylor, Byrd. *I'm in Charge of Celebrations.* Bt Bound, 1999. Hardcover (LB): ISBN 0-785-78338-5.

How often do students complain, "Nothing ever happens to me! I have nothing interesting to write about!" In this magical book, everyday happenings are transformed into moments of personal celebration. The heroine of this enchanting story loses herself in the wonder of a summer meteor shower, ventures closer than ever before to a timid coyote, revels in wildflowers, dances with the dust devils, and discovers that clouds can come in surprising colors—all cause for personal celebration. A story that will help your students discover the celebrational moments in their lives, too.

Baylor, Byrd. *The Other Way To Listen.* Bt Bound, 1999. Hardcover (LB): ISBN 0-613-05642-6.

"When you know 'the other way to listen,' you can hear wildflower seeds burst open, you can hear the rocks murmuring, and the hills singing, and it seems like the most natural thing in the world. Of course it takes a lot of practice, and you can't be in a hurry." I love this book; I love all of Byrd Baylor's books. They soothe me; they help me take deeper, more thoughtful breaths; they help me to reflect on the important things in life. In this piece, the very act of listening is transformed to reflect the essence of the natural world. As with all her works, nature is the central character and we are invited along for the ride. (YA)

Bercaw, Edna Coe. ***Halmoni's Day.*** Dial Books, 2000. Hardcover (LB): ISBN 0-8037-2444-6.
Grandparents' Day at school is always exciting, but for Jennifer it has worries, too. Her grand-mother is visiting from South Korea. So, as well as the language difference, she is concerned about what her grandmother will say to the class as she receives her special award. She need not have worried. Grandmother's talk to the class about when she was a child is so captivating nobody even notices the bell for lunchtime. A gentle story of family that will capture the heart.

Berger, Barbara Helen. ***All the Way to Lhasa: A Tale From Tibet.*** Philomel Books, 2002.
Hardcover (LB): ISBN 0-399-23387-3.
Young listeners will recognize the "Tortoise and the Hare" moral of this story about a boy and his yak walking over the mountains to the Tibetan holy city of Lhasa. Evocative illustrations add an atmosphere of reverence and calm to this unusual book. Also good for the trait of sentence fluency.

Blake, Quentin. ***Loveykins.*** Peachtree Publishers, 2003. Hardcover: ISBN 1-561-45282-3.
Finding a baby bird brings out the motherly instincts in Angela. But it takes a destructive storm to make her realize that for some creatures, kindness means setting them free to face whatever may come. This story provides a tongue-in-cheek lesson about responsibility.

Bottner, Barbara. ***The Scaredy Cats.*** Simon & Schuster, 2003. Hardcover: ISBN 0-689-83786-0.
The scaredy cat family is so scared of everything that they end up doing nothing, which leads to worry, frustration, and boredom. But the youngest member of the family finally realizes that if bad things can happen, so can good things … and life changes for the better. A simple story that exemplifies profound wisdom about unfounded fears and the paralysis that can result.

Bridges, Shirin Yim. ***Ruby's Wish.*** Chronicle Books, 2002. Hardcover: ISBN 0-8118-3490-5.
Written in simple language, this true story carries a profound lesson in equality and determination. Set in old China, we encounter a little girl who is unlike any of her many sisters in this large household. Rather than getting married, Ruby has her mind set on going to university. But girls are supposed to learn how to run a house, so she has to work twice as hard as the boys to keep up with her studies as well as the expected tasks of sewing and cooking and keeping house. Can she persuade anyone, particularly her grandfather, to listen to her dream? Illustrations by Sophie Blackall capture just the right atmosphere.

Brumbeau, Jeff. ***Miss Hunnicutt's Hat.*** Orchard Books, 2003. Hardcover: ISBN 0-439-31895-5.
The staid and proper Miss Hunnicutt usually behaves the way that is expected in the staid and proper town of Littleton. But on the day of the Queen's visit she decides to wear her new hat from Paris. And so begins this colorful and humorous tale of tolerance and courage in the face of not-so-subtle pressure to conform. Older listeners will relate to the messages of peer pressure and respect for individual differences. (YA)

Burdett, Lois. *A Child's Portrait of Shakespeare.* Firefly Books, 1995.
Hardcover (LB): ISBN 0-88753-263-2.

How do you make the world of Shakespeare accessible to readers as young as seven? Lois Burdett will show you in this amazing work. At the heart is a rhyming couplet version of Shakespeare's life and times. In response, Burdett's young students have drawn portraits of the Bard, his parents, his children, his city, and the Globe Theater. They have totally immersed themselves in Shakespeare's language and world vision by writing diary and journal entries, taking on the roles of Shakespeare and the major players in his life, drafting "in character" letters to one another, reflecting on 1600s history (the evils of the Black Plague) and, generally, transporting themselves right into the spirit of the times. Through their full-color art and their insightful (often wildly humorous) writing, we are privileged to witness their profound understanding of Shakespeare's work and of why it still touches our hearts and minds today. As one student (Christian) put it, "If Shakespeare were alive today, I would invite him to sleep over in my tree fort and we would talk a lot about his plays."

Burdett, Lois. *Macbeth for Kids.* Black Moss Press, 1997. Hardcover (LB): ISBN 0-88753-287-X.

Macbeth what is the matter with you? It is your imaginashon! Do you want the banquet to be totally rooined? Relax! Behave yourself. You are embarasing me. You call yourself a man? More like a cowerdly snake! Now pull yourself together! —Lady Macbeth (Matt Hunt, age 7)

In letters like this one, in pictures, diaries, and reflective writings, we are taken inside second-grade students' responses to and interpretations of Macbeth, a work that clearly holds them spellbound. As in her other books, Lois Burdett retells the play in rhyming couplets, helping students follow the plot, understand the characters' motivations, and bring their own meanings to the text. Sixty-four wonderful pages of Burdett's charming poetry complemented by her students' writing and delightful illustrations will make you wish you could rush out now to the nearest production of *Macbeth*—and take one of Burdett's students along to help you make sense of it all: "I think SHAKESPEARE wrote the Scottish play to tell the people that bad doesn't pay and that what goes around comes around" (Matt, age 7).

Burdett, Lois. *Twelfth Night for Kids.* Bt Bound, 1995. Hardcover: ISBN 0-61351-192-1.

Will Sir Toby Belch and Maria resolve their differences? Will the beautiful Olivia and Sebastian find true love? Or will Duke Orsino win Olivia's heart? Will the many mistaken identities sort themselves out or lead to chaos, turmoil, and heartbreak? It's a comedy of secret notes, disguises, plots, and plans, Shakespeare style, and Lois Burdett's imaginative second-grade writers and illustrators are well up to the task of helping us all visualize and enjoy the tale. Was Shakespeare always this much fun, or is it Burdett's rhyming couplets and her students' engaging, inspired responses that make the magic happen? A little of each, perhaps. Let the wisdom of second-graders help you see Shakespeare with renewed insight. As Jeff tells us, "I know why he called it Twelfth Night. He had to write it at twelve o'clock at night cause none of his kids were around to bug him."

Cain, Sheridan. *The Crunching, Munching Caterpillar.* Tiger Tales, 2003.
Hardcover: ISBN 1-58925-025-7.

Caterpillar spends his days crunching and munching on green leaves, but he is envious of the bee and the sparrow who can fly. Only butterfly knows that caterpillar will eventually get his wish. A colorfully illustrated introduction to life cycles in nature for younger listeners.

Cannon, Ann. *I Know What You Do When I Go to School.* Bt Bound, 2001.
Hardcover: ISBN 0-613-52575-2.

Here's a clever piece of prose! What really happens back at home when kids go to school? Are there soap bubbles and fabulous parties? Are there amazing dinosaur discoveries? Do sheets and towels turn into incredible and fantastic forts? Join in as Howie invents many fanciful stories about what happens at home while he is away at school. He uses his vivid imagination in an attempt to convince his mother to let him stay home and have fun with her and his little brother. This book would be a great prompt for imaginative writing and student recreation of the central idea! (Hey—I wonder what my cats are up to at my house right now!)

Cannon, Janell. *Verdi.* Harcourt Brace, 1997. Hardcover (LB): ISBN 0-15-201028-9.

The author of the much loved *Stellaluna* has hit the bull's eye again! In this exquisitely illustrated book (also drawn by Cannon) Verdi learns the very painful lessons of growing up, fitting in, and finding a place for himself. This is a compassionate piece, filled with gentle humor and insight. As an added bonus, there are several pages at the end of the story with factual information about snakes. Students who read this book will easily understand how research and story writing connect.

Chambers, Veronica. *Amistad Rising: A Story of Freedom.* Raintree/Steck Vaughn, 1998.
Hardcover (LB): ISBN 0-817-25510-9.

This is the true story of Joseph Cinque's fight for freedom after being kidnapped and imprisoned on a slave ship headed for Cuba. We experience the appalling conditions under which slaves were transported to the new world in the early 19th century, and the frustration that Cinque and his companions felt as they first won their freedom but then found themselves back in prison. A salutary tale for students studying the early days of the abolitionist movement. (YA)

Cherry, Lynne. *The Armadillo From Amarillo.* Gulliver Green (Harcourt Brace), 1994.
Hardcover: ISBN 0-15-200359-2.

Have you ever asked yourself, "Where in the world am I?" Sasparillo, the armadillo in this story, both written and illustrated by the amazingly talented Lynne Cherry, asks that question over and over as he seeks to find his place in the big, wide world. He begins in the wide open expanse of Texas and page by page, detail by detail, he comes to understand that what he knows, his "place," is part of a much bigger world. Each picture and the text that accompanies it in this finely written and illustrated piece underscores the theme of self-discovery. The story is about the journey to understand more about how the individual can relate to the bigness of what is out there—a challenge to explore and learn as much as we can during the course of our lives. Lynne Cherry herself says it best at the end in her thoughtfully written author's note: "The story is meant to inspire you to be interested in discovering where in the world you are. Sasparillo learns that the world he knows in the tangled woods is just one of many. You can learn about where you are by reading books, looking at maps, … and someday setting off to see the world." P.S. Don't miss *The Great Kapok Tree,* and *A River Ran Wild* for other books drawing upon Lynne Cherry's passion for appreciating and understanding the importance of finding a balance that supports man's life on earth without destroying the environment.

Cherry, Lynne. *The Dragon and the Unicorn.* Gulliver Green Books (Harcourt Brace), 1995.
Hardcover (LB): ISBN 0-15-224193-0.

I love this book. Perhaps it is the use of an original fairy tale to tell such an important story; perhaps it is the appeal of the characters—the dragon Valerio, the unicorn Allegra, or the king's daughter Arianna; perhaps it is the gentle but powerful theme of protecting the environment and respecting all the living creatures on earth. I'm not sure. All I know is this piece works. It is a wake-up call that not only reminds us to honor the history of the earth and the sensitive balance needed for it to survive, but it also teaches us respect. The characters, though magical and steeped in mythology, seem very real. I wanted to read more about them long after the story was finished. The text is very eloquent in its simplicity. At the beginning, the sentences are simple and straightforward. As the story becomes more complex, so does the very structure of the language as it moves the reader carefully through the piece to its ultimate conclusion. The ending parallels the beginning by a return to the simpler rhythm and flow of ideas: "The Ardet Forest remains a haven for all living things. For people, it is a place to find peace and silence. But for animals, and for the dragon and the unicorn, it is home." Well said, Lynne, well said. Wouldn't it be a great idea to read this book to your students and let them find their own issues about the environment, which could be researched and told through stories like those of Lynne Cherry? (YA)

Cherry, Lynne. *Flute's Journey: The Life of a Wood Thrush.*
Gulliver Green Books (Harcourt Brace), 1997.
Hardcover (LB): ISBN 0-15-292853-7.

In another terrific piece by Lynne Cherry, this time she chooses to tell the story of the wood thrush and its struggle for survival. In this incredibly well-researched story, the reader gets an indepth understanding of the perils facing the wood thrush and what must happen in order to protect this species. As an added bonus, Lynne tells the story behind the story of *Flute's Journey* at the end. Kids and adults will be moved and feel the "call to action" after reading this book from Lynne's powerful environmental series. (YA)

Cherry, Lynne, and Plotkin, Mark J. *The Shaman's Apprentice.* Harcourt Brace, 1998.
Hardcover (LB): ISBN 0-15-201281-8.

Combining science and history, this beautifully illustrated book depicts the clash of cultures when Europeans encounter the indigenous peoples of the Amazon rain forest. The gentle story belies the catastrophic effects of introduced diseases among native peoples, and illustrates the irony contained in the sources of life-saving medicines. A good example of how the narrative genre can be used by content area teachers and students. (YA)

Clary, Margie Willis. *A Sweet, Sweet Basket.* Sandlapper, 1995. Hardcover: ISBN 0-87844-127.

A gift from the wonderful teachers and staff in Richland District Two, South Carolina, this book is a model for students as they learn to weave factual information into a piece of prose that is accurate, interesting, and thoughtful. If you don't know the history of the sweetgrass baskets found in the marketplace in Charleston, you'll enjoy this story of the great heritage that is represented in the artful craft of basket weaving. If you are familiar with sweetgrass baskets, walking through the pages of their history will give you a renewed appreciation for the traditions that they represent.

Cole, Joanna. *The Magic School Bus: At the Waterworks.* Bt Bound, 1999.
Hardcover (LB): ISBN 0-833-51744-9.
> Meet Ms. Frizzle, "the strangest teacher in the school." But boy, oh boy, does she know how to throw a field trip. The world is her classroom; no place is too difficult to seek out. And when she takes her class on a tour of the city waterworks, she does not tell them to stay clean and dry—and she provides the SCUBA gear. You just have to love a teacher like that. This book is one of a series, all packed with facts, adventure, humor, voice, and some of the greatest illustrations ever. An excellent example of how much little details matter. (Another favorite: *The Magic School Bus: Lost in the Solar System.*)

Coles, Robert. *The Story of Ruby Bridges.* Scholastic, 1995. Hardcover (LB): ISBN 0-590-57281-4.
> A gift from my wonderful friend Debbie Stewart of Topeka, Kansas, this nonfiction piece chronicles the story of Ruby Bridges, the first black child to attend an all-white elementary school. It's a familiar story to some, but it deserves a place in all our classrooms not only as a nicely written piece, but as a slice of U.S. history that is important for every child to study and reflect upon. The lessons of forgiveness, appreciation, and understanding are applicable every single day in all our schools and classrooms.

Cooney, Barbara. *Miss Rumphius.* Viking Press, 1982. Hardcover (LB): ISBN 0-67-047958-6.
> "Alice Rumphius wanted to travel the world when she grew up, and then to live by the sea—just as her grandfather had done. But there is one more thing, he tells her: She must do something to make the world more beautiful. Young Alice does not yet know what that will be …." In this charming Victorian story, readers are invited to explore all the ways a person could make the world more beautiful. A great story starter idea for writers of all ages. (American Book Award winner)

Coyle, Carmela LaVigna. *Do Princesses Wear Hiking Boots?* Rising Moon, 2003.
Hardcover: ISBN 0-873-58828-2.
> … Only when they take the scenic routes! Moms (and dads) will relate to this book, built upon a series of questions from an obviously emancipated young lady. The answers, of course, lie within ourselves; which is the final message of the story, and one worth repeating over and over.

Cronin, Doreen. *Click, Clack, Moo: Cows That Type.* Simon and Schuster, 2000.
Hardcover: ISBN 0-689-83213-3.
> Farmer Brown is amazed when he hears his cows clickety clacking on a typewriter. But that is only the beginning of his problems in this humorous, tongue-in-cheek story of demands, strikes, and compromise. Colorful drawings enhance the fun.

Daly, Niki. *Once Upon a Time.* Farrar, Straus and Giroux, 2003. Hardcover: ISBN 0-374-35633-5.
> The biggest challenge in Sarie's young life is not the long, dusty walk to school each day under a hot South African sun, but the trial of having to read aloud in front of the class. This changes when Sarie and her Aunt Anna find a magical old book in their rusted car. Reading the old book with her aunt gradually increases Sarie's confidence and skill, until reading in school becomes a joy. Children who find the task of reading difficult will relate to this tale, and perhaps find some inspiration in its message.

De Beer, Hans. ***The Little Polar Bear and the Big Balloon.*** North-South Books, 2002. Hardcover (LB): ISBN 0-7358-1533-X.

> Lars, the little polar bear, finds he has taken on more than he can handle when he tries to help out an oil-covered puffin. This experience finally convinces him that keeping four paws on the ground is a good idea for a young bear. Beautiful illustrations accompany this tale of friendship and caring for others.

DeFelice, Cynthia. ***The Real, True Dulcie Campbell.*** Farrar, Straus and Giroux, 2002. Hardcover: ISBN 0-374-36220-3.

> Dulcie Campbell, who lives on a farm in Iowa, is convinced that she is really a princess misplaced at birth. Her daydreams turn sour, however, as she reads fairy tales of kissing frogs and wicked fairies, terrible trolls and carnivorous ogres. She decides that the reality of "ordinary" life is much safer and more comfortable. A cautionary tale about wishing for greener pastures.

Dragonwagon, Crescent. ***Home Place.*** Aladdin Books, 1999. Hardcover (LB): ISBN 0-785-71398-0.

> This beautifully written and illustrated story is about a deserted house in the woods that is rediscovered by a family out for a hike. The young girl fantasizes about who might have lived there, and when she does so she recreates a whole family and their history to go with the now-deserted home. The text is lyrical and weaves two cultures together through their love and appreciation of the daffodils, the family suppers, and the honeysuckle-vined chimney. A nice choice to share for imagining, revisioning, and re-seeing in another time and culture.

English, Karen. ***Nadia's Hands.*** Boyds Mill Press, 1999. Hardcover (LB): ISBN 1-56397-667-6. Being the flower girl at a traditional Pakistani wedding means having orange-colored *mehndi* on the hands, but Nadia—the chosen one—is not sure she is ready to face her classmates on Monday with the coloring still there. Yet through the wedding ceremony and later in the presence of relatives at the reception, she comes to realize that the *mehndi* is part of her heritage and something to show with pride. An empathetic description of practices and traditions that have become part of our own culture.

Everett, Gwen. ***Li'l Sis and Uncle Willie.*** Rizzoli, 1992. Hardcover: ISBN 0-8478-1462-9. Based on the life and paintings of William H. Johnson, this true story examines the impact of art, paintings, and family relationships as a young girl discovers how big the world can be. It is an inspirational book that celebrates cultural differences and validates the idea that important stories come from trying to make sense of our own personal experiences.

Falconer, Ian. ***Olivia Saves the Circus.*** Atheneum, 2001. Hardcover: ISBN 0-689-82954-X. Olivia's trip to the circus turns into an adventure of mammoth proportions—at least in her imagination. But it makes for a pretty exciting "show and tell" at school, nevertheless. Ian Falconer's two-tone illustrations add to the humor of this clever story.

Fleischman, Paul. ***Weslandia.*** Candlewick Press, 1999. Hardcover (LB): ISBN 0-7636-0006-7.
Wesley is the classic outsider: intelligent, nonconformist, and shunned by his peers. So he decides that summer vacation is the time to do something really grand—found his own civilization! You will be awed by the creative ingenuity that goes into turning a summer project into something really special. A great book to encourage older listeners to think "outside the box." (YA)

Fletcher, Ralph. ***Grandpa Never Lies.*** Clarion Books, 2000. Hardcover (LB): ISBN 0-395-79770-5.
Listening to Grandpa's magical explanations of ordinary things is the best of times, especially when visiting his little cabin in the woods. This lyrical description of a child's relationship with her grandfather borders on the poetic. Also good for voice.

Fox, Mem. ***Wilfrid Gordon McDonald Partridge.*** Kane/Miller, 1985.
Hardcover: ISBN 0-916-291-04-9.
Young writers often have a hard time thinking of ways to bring personal meaning to everyday objects or experiences. As teachers, we yearn for the moments of insight that separate personal experiences from the story or paper with only the obvious retelling. In *Wilfrid Gordon …* (named after her father), Mem Fox shows how everyday objects can trigger very personal and special remembrances for an older woman who has lost her memory.

Fraser, Mary Ann. ***IQ Goes to the Library.*** Walker & Co., 2003.
Hardcover (LB): ISBN 0-8027-8878-5.
IQ spends Library Week discovering the treasures of the school library. But he is worried that he won't get his permission sheet signed and be able to check out a book before the end of the week. Only a last-minute scramble and the wonders of technology can save the day. Use this story to build the anticipation of young listeners for a visit to the school library.

Frasier, Debra. ***On the Day You Were Born.*** Harcourt Brace, 1991.
Hardcover (LB): ISBN 0-15-257995-8.
"On the day you were born the round planet Earth turned toward your morning sky, whirling past darkness, spinning the night into light." In this beautiful and reverent text, author Debra Frasier combines a warmly personal voice with a global sense of time and space. Frasier's poetic prose engagingly celebrates the coming of new life all the while gently probing the mysteries of Earth's rotation, the force of gravity, the warmth and energy-giving force of the sun, animal migration, the pull of the tides, falling rain, the growth of trees, the rush of wind, and the evolution of human diversity. The initial text glorifies the specialness of birth; a wondrously informative prose appendix expands and illuminates themes just touched on in the earlier poetic tribute. A matchless example of how to pack a lot of information into a few eloquent words. (Parents' Choice Award winner)

Gay, Marie-Louise. ***Stella, Fairy of the Forest.*** Groundwood Books, 2002.
Hardcover: ISBN 0-88899-448-6.
Stella's younger brother Sam has many questions about the forest, some of which even Stella is hard-pressed to answer. But one thing they do agree on is the wish that catching sight of a fairy has given them. A cute introduction to the forest for young listeners.

Gilles, Almira Astudillo. ***Willie Wins.*** Lee and Low Books, 2001.
Hardcover (LB): ISBN 1-58430-023-X.

    Willie's day goes from bad to worse when, after a losing baseball game, his Dad gives him an *alkansiya*—a coconut—to use as a piggy bank for school. The bank is the most unusual in the class, but Willie is determined to tough out even the chiding comments of class bully Stan in order to win the class competition and discover what the secret content of the *alkansiya* is. The story not only illustrates the rewards of patience and determination, but lends itself to raising the thorny issue of emotional bullying.

Henkes, Kevin. ***Wemberly Worried.*** Greenwillow Books, 2000.
Hardcover (LB) : ISBN 0-688-17028-5.

    Wemberly worries about anything and everything. Until, that is, she starts school and finds that there is just too much exciting activity going on to be worried as well. Young listeners will relate to Wemberly's concerns.

Hepworth, Catherine. ***Antics!*** Putnam, 1992.
Paperback: ISBN 0-399-21862-9.

    This hilarious ABC book is a great example of how students can take any topic, gather significant information about it, and then turn it into a cleverly formatted ABC book. You might want to consider using this book under the trait of word choice, also, because the vocabulary sparkles. I bet you'd never dream how fascinating the world of ants really is!

Hest, Amy. ***When Jessie Came Across the Sea.*** Candlewick Press, 1997.
Hardcover: ISBN 0-7636-0094-6.

    This is a poignant story of the hope and courage shown by immigrants as they left behind the known and familiar to establish a new life in the United States. Jessie is the fortunate recipient of a ticket across the Atlantic from Europe. Despite her new life and new friendships, she does not forget her obligation to her grandmother back in the old country. An inspiring story for older listeners. (Christopher Award winner; YA)

James, Simon. ***Dear Mr. Blueberry.*** Margaret K. McElderry Books, 1991.
Hardcover (LB): ISBN 0-689-50529-9.

    Looking for a way to share information in a new format? In *Dear Mr. Blueberry,* Emily writes to her science teacher about the blue whale she thinks is in her pond at home, asking for advice on what to feed it and how to take care of it. Her teacher writes back, gently explaining that the animal in her pond couldn't possibly be a whale and why. In the letters that follow, Emily is more and more adamant about the existence of the blue whale, while the science teacher tries harder and harder to teach her why that could not possibly be so. This format for sharing information inspires imagination and creativity, and could apply to any subject or grade.

Johnson, D.B. *Henry Climbs a Mountain.* Houghton Mifflin, 2003.
Hardcover (LB): ISBN 0-618-26902-9.
> Based on the life of Henry David Thoreau, this lighthearted story packs a substantial message about social change, the power of ideas, and imagination. A conversation starter for listeners of many different age groups. (YA)

Johnson, Stephen T. *Alphabet City.* Viking Press, 1996. Hardcover (LB): ISBN 0-670-85631-2.
> This book is an illustrated tour of the lines, shapes, and forms found in our world. But more than that, it features all the letters of the alphabet—all you have to do to see them is to look at things through the eyes of an artist. Begin your adventure with the foreword by illustrator Stephen Johnson who says, "I hope that my paintings will inspire children and adults to look at their surroundings in a fresh and playful way." I don't think I'll ever look at a confluence of buildings again without trying to see if a letter is formed where they meet the skyline.

Johnston, Tony. *Day of the Dead.* Harcourt Brace, 1997. Hardcover (LB): ISBN 0-15-222863-2.
> As students learn to acknowledge and celebrate their own cultural traditions, this little book might serve as a good example of explaining one such Mexican celebration, the annual *El Dia de Los Muertos,* the Day of the Dead. This book opens as a small town in Mexico begins preparations for the celebration and moves through events of the day, and into the night as the townspeople walk to the graveyards to welcome the spirits of loved ones home again. As a writing/personal research assignment or research paper idea, students might enjoy exploring their own cultural celebrations and comparing one to the other for similarities and differences. (A nice companion piece would be *My House Has Stars* by Megan McDonald, under the trait of voice.)

Kimmel, Eric A. *The Greatest of All.* Holiday House, 1991. Hardcover: ISBN 0-8234-0885-X.
> When Chuko mouse tells her father she wishes to marry another mouse, it takes him a while to come to terms with the idea. And then it is only after talking to the Sun, Wind, and the Emperor himself. This Japanese folktale reinforces the idea that our greatest need can often be satisfied at home. (YA)

Kimmel, Eric A. *ZigaZak! A Magical Hannukah Night.* Doubleday, 2001.
Hardcover (LB): ISBN 0-385-32652-1.
> In this Hanukkah story, two little devils decide to turn a celebration into a misery. But they did not reckon with the local rabbi who, intent on finding the good in everyone, turns misfortune into the best celebration anyone in the town could remember. The tale, whose underlying message is to look for the good in everything and everybody, has significance for all of us. Also good for the trait of word choice.

Kramer, Stephen P. *Lightning.* Carolrhoda Books, 1992. Hardcover: ISBN 0-87614-659-0.
> Fact-based expository writing doesn't have to be sluggish and boring. Steve Kramer's book is jam-packed with details and information, yet holds your attention as well as any other well-crafted story. And oh, those photographs! Wow!

Krull, Kathleen. *Harvesting Hope: The Story of Cesar Chavez.* Harcourt, 2003.
Hardcover (LB): ISBN 0-15-201437-3.

A powerful story, powerfully written, is of one man's struggle for equity and a decent way of life in the face of enormous odds. Chavez followed in the footprints of Gandhi and Martin Luther King Jr. in calling for nonviolent protest to gain attention for the plight of migrant farm workers. Pitted against overwhelming business interests, he created a grassroots movement that eventually changed laws and the lives of thousands of workers who produce America's fruits and vegetables. Illustrations by Yuri Morakles beautifully capture the atmosphere of this struggle. (YA)

Lakin, Patricia. *Dad and Me in the Morning.* Albert Whitman, 1994.
Hardcover (LB): ISBN0-8075-1419-5.

With hearing loss as a factor, this is the story of the date that a father and his son have to go out at dawn to watch the sun rise over the sea. They are not disappointed as it turns in minutes from a sliver on the horizon to a massive ball in the sky. A simple pleasure told and illustrated with loving simplicity. Also good for the trait of word choice.

Lambert, Martha. *I Won't Get Lost.* HarperCollins, 2003. Hardcover: ISBN 0-06-028960-0.
Horatio likes most things at school, and those he doesn't like he ignores completely. This unfortunate habit has disastrous results when he tries to find his way home one evening. A great story to impress younger listeners with the need for careful listening, and knowing personal information.

Langen, Annette. *Letters From Felix.* Abbeville Press, 1994. Hardcover: ISBN 1-55859-886-3.
A little stuffed rabbit is inadvertently left behind as the family packs and heads home after vacation. What happens next is the cleverly told adventure of the rabbit as it tries to find its way home. The book utilizes lots of forms of organization and formatting by including postcards, letters, and notes that open and can be read as Felix the bunny travels the world. Pretty great idea … reminiscent of the *Jolly Postman* series. Students of all ages can recreate travel adventures to places they are studying in social studies. Or, perhaps they can plan a world tour of their own and write letters and postcards to make their own book by combining writing and geography. Can you think of other possibilities?

Lears, Laurie. *Becky the Brave: A Story About Epilepsy.* Albert Whitman, 2002.
Hardcover (LB): ISBN0-8075-0601-X.

Dealing with the issues of epilepsy is difficult at any age, but for Becky—on the edge of adolescence—it is devastating. She is constantly afraid of the impact that witnessing a seizure might have on her friends and classmates. When the inevitable happens she retreats to her bed, but it is the courage of her younger sister and the understanding of her teacher and class that pulls her through. A touching cry for empathy.

Lears, Laurie. *Ben Has Something To Say: A Story About Stuttering.* Albert Whitman, 2000.
Hardcover: ISBN 0-8075-0633-8.

Ben avoids talking to anyone outside his family to cover up his stuttering. But his love for guard dog Spike, soon to go to the pound, forces him to confront his fears and make the effort to talk in defense of his animal buddy. Ben learns that what he says is more important than how he says it, and reflecting this message with patience and understanding is the best way that listeners can help those who stutter.

Lesser, Carolyn. *Great Crystal Bear.* Harcourt Brace, 1996. Hardcover (LB): ISBN 0-15-200667-2.
What do you know about polar bears? They're big. They're white. They hibernate in the winter. They live in the Arctic. (Is that the North Pole or the South Pole?) What else? If you are like most people, adults or children, that's about it. And there is more, so much more that we will find fascinating about these magnificent creatures in *Great Crystal Bear.* For instance, did you know these Arctic bears have black skin? Do you know the Inuit legend about Nanuk—how a man entered an igloo and emerged as a bear, dressed in fur? Do you know what they eat? Or how they survive the great storms? How is it that they leave only one set of prints—front and back in the same place as they trek across the tundra? So many interesting things to learn about the great bear—and all woven tightly and artfully into this short expository picture book. The text creates the opportunity for us to appreciate survival, beauty, and wisdom. It allows us to wonder.

Lewis, Paul Owen. *Grasper.* Beyond Words, 1993. Hardcover: ISBN 0-941831-85-X.
Many students will immediately relate to this tale of Grasper, a small and unenlightened crab who lives in a cramped and overcrowded tide pool. Like Grasper, most of us discover the world is bigger and better than we ever dared imagine as young children; but we also find that it can be dangerous, too. This delightfully told metaphor for the process of growing up is one that should become an instant favorite for perceptive readers of all ages.

Lewis, Paul Owen. *The Jupiter Stone.* Tricycle Press, 2003. Hardcover: ISBN 1-58246-107-4.
A small striped rock provides an example of the meaning of infinity in this beautifully illustrated book. Falling to Earth in its infancy, the rock is eventually picked up and returned to space, only to be found and begin a new journey. A wonderful way to introduce younger listeners to the concepts of cycles and space. Also great for organization.

Lionni, Leo. *The Greentail Mouse.* Alfred A. Knopf, 2001 (re-issue).
Hardcover (LB): ISBN 0-37592-399-3.
Encouraged by a visiting city mouse, a community of field mice organizes its own "Fat Tuesday," only to find that donning scary masks can turn a peaceful place into a place of threat and fear. A cautionary tale about what is and is not real, and being able to see the difference. Also good for the trait of organization.

Lobel, Arnold. *Fables.* HarperCollins, 1980. Hardcover (LB): ISBN 0-06-023974-3.
Good stories always make a point. Lobel blends wry humor and beguiling simplicity to hold the eye and ear of even the youngest listener while bringing a smile to adult faces, too. It's no small trick and no one does it better. Twenty short but punchy tales run a short page apiece—fine for reading aloud when time is limited. A classic. (Caldecott Award winner)

Lobel, Gillian. *Does Anybody Love Me?* Good Books, 2002. Hardcover: ISBN 1-56148-368-0.
Charlie runs into trouble with mom and dad over her creative games, so she decides to run away to the jungle with her loyal buddy Panda. But the jungle has drawbacks: There is nothing to drink, no shelter from the rain, and it is dark. So, how to return home with pride intact? Maybe grandpa can provide a solution. A story that captures feelings younger listeners will recognize. Also good for the trait of organization.

Loupy, Christophe. *Don't Worry, Wags.* North South Books, 2003.
Hardcover (LB): ISBN 0-7358-1850-9.

> Wags is worried by everything—burrowing in haystacks, splashing in puddles, and especially taking a trip to farmers' market. Her fears seem to be coming true when she finds herself separated from her family and alone. But around every dark cloud is a silver lining, and this story is no exception. A great book for encouraging youngsters to face their fears.

Lunge-Larsen, Lise. *The Race of the Birkebeiners.* Houghton Mifflin, 2001.
Hardcover: ISBN 0-618-10313-9.

> An unusual saga that has come down to us from 800 years ago, it tells the story of how Prince Hakon was saved from the rich Baglers to become king and bring an era of peace and prosperity to Norway. The engrossing tale is enhanced by unusual woodcut illustrations. Also good for the trait of word choice.

Macaulay, David. *Angelo.* Houghton Mifflin, 2002. Hardcover: ISBN 0-618-16826-5.

> Angelo spends his life restoring the plaster facades of buildings and sculptures, but his masterpiece is the front of an old church. He is accompanied in his work by a pet pigeon. His final act is to provide a permanent home for his faithful friend in an appropriate place. A poignant story of kindness and friendship. Also good for the trait of sentence fluency.

Macaulay, David. *Motel of the Mysteries.* Houghton Mifflin, 1988.
Hardcover: ISBN 0-395-28424-4.

> It is the year 4022; all of the ancient country of Usa has been buried under many feet of third- and fourth-class junk mail during a catastrophe that occurred back in 1985. Imagine, then, the excitement that Howard Carson, an amateur archaeologist, experienced when, in crossing the perimeter of an abandoned excavation site, he felt the ground give way beneath him and found himself at the bottom of a shaft which, judging from the DO NOT DISTURB sign hanging from an archaic doorknob, was clearly the entrance to a still-sealed burial chamber. Actually, the site is an old motel. As Howard Carson proceeds to label every artifact erroneously and draw hilarious conclusions about what he discovers, readers are invited to think how they, too, might become amateur archaeologists, piecing together vividly real characters from the artifacts they leave behind. (YA)

MacDonald, Ross. *Another Perfect Day.* Roaring Book Press, 2002.
Hardcover (LB): ISBN 0-7613-2659-6.

> Jack's day starts beautifully, but quickly goes downhill until he learns the proper way to … wake up! Illustrated in the style of 1940s comic books, this story has a not-so-subtle humor that will have you giggling all the way through to the twist at the end.

MacLachlan, Patricia. *All the Places To Love.* HarperCollins, 1994. Hardcover (LB): 0-06-021099-0.

> What an extraordinary find! This book belongs on all teachers' shelves as they work with kids to help them find the important topics to write about that come from their everyday world—the world that truly matters to them. In this tender piece, a youngster recalls each time initials were carved into the barn rafters signifying the birth of a new child in the family. Gentle, sensitive, personal—this piece has moments of grandeur written into every page. (YA)

Magdanz, James. *Go Home, River.* Alaska Northwest Books, 1996.
Hardcover: ISBN 0-88240-476-8.
> The traditions of the Coastal Indian tribes are a part of the local culture and lore in the Pacific Northwest. This piece, historically accurate and entertaining (a rare combination), is the story of a young Alaska Eskimo boy as he explores a river from its mountainous beginnings to its eventual terminating point in the delta. The journey is one of self-discovery for the main character (never named) as well, and readers will find themselves drawn into each part of this unique and reverent story. Use this piece to teach Alaska history, Eskimo culture, the water cycle, and geography. Use it to show how accurate information can be woven into the context of a story. Use it to help students understand their own personal journeys of discovery.

Mak, Kam. *My Chinatown.* HarperCollins, 2002. Hardcover (LB): ISBN 0-06-029191-5.
> Chinatown is home to one small boy who in the cycle of seasons learns to appreciate the juiciness of kumquats, the craft in making a pair of shoes, the sweetness of a bird's song, and the exciting beat of a dragon boat race. Join him on a poetic journey of discovery into a culture transported to strange shores, but which is now home. Also excellent for sentence fluency and voice.

Marshall, Rita. *I Hate To Read!* Creative Education, 1992. Hardcover (LB): ISBN 0-88682-531-8.
> OK, OK, I'll admit it. I bought this book because of the title, but it turned out to be a real gem. Third-grader Victor Dickens goes out of his way to avoid books, but one day, he inadvertently looks at a book and the characters become so real for him that he begins to care and turn the pages, and—zap!—we got him!

Martin, Rafe. *The Storytelling Princess.* Putnam, 2001. Hardcover (LB): ISBN 0-39-922924-8.
> This clever story is about an independent prince and princess, each of whom is determined not to marry the person chosen by their parents. But fate lends a hand, and they discover the one they love is the one chosen for them. Listeners will relate to the strong-willed stand against authority that these two young characters portray. (YA)

Mathers, Petra. *Sophie and Lou.* HarperCollins, 1999. Hardcover (LB): ISBN 0-06-4433331-5.
> Love stories just don't come much more endearing than this. Sophie, who is painfully shy, learns to dance in the safety of her own cozy home, peeking wistfully through the window at the Kick Up Your Heels dance studio across the street. Soon, inspired by her newfound agility, Sophie is swinging with the best of them and dreaming of new dancing shoes. She meets the infatuated and gentle Lou, and the rest is history. A beautiful way to explore the themes of overcoming shyness and helping one's inner self to blossom.

McClintock, Barbara. *Dahlia.* Frances Foster, 2002. Hardcover: ISBN 0-374-31678-3.
> When the new doll Dahlia arrives, Charlotte forcibly points out that she will be expected to play hard despite her lace frills and silk ribbons. But Dahlia proves to be as tough as can be, and quickly becomes Charlotte's best friend. A clever story of friendship and acceptance, supported by a classic style of illustration. Also good for the trait of organization.

McLerran, Alice. ***Roxaboxen.*** HarperCollins, 1991. Hardcover (LB): ISBN 0-688-07593-2.
This story is based on events that really happened to Alice McLerran's mother. The author has recreated the magical world her mother and relatives describe in letters, diaries, and maps. She presents us with "a celebration of the active imagination, of the ability of children to create, even with the most unpromising materials, a world of fantasy so real and multidimensional that it earns a lasting place in memory." This is *Roxaboxen,* a reminder that writing should tap this creative spark and be allowed to roam free. Perhaps your students have created a memorable place like Roxaboxen and are ready to write about it—or maybe this could be the beginning of other imaginary and special places.

Morrissey, Dean. ***The Great Kettles: A Tale of Time.*** Harry N. Abrams, 1997.
Hardcover: ISBN 0-8109-3396-9.
The young hero from Morrissey's first book *Ship of Dreams* returns in this tale of time travel. Joey builds a makeshift time machine from the instructions in an old book he finds in his attic. But never in his wildest dreams did he imagine that the machine would actually succeed in casting him back to a place where time begins. Dean Morrissey's story is brilliantly enhanced by his minutely detailed illustrations.

Moss, Marissa. ***Amelia's Notebook.*** Bt Bound, 1999. Hardcover (LB): ISBN 0-613-15708-7.
Here's a book that just cries out, "Pick me up!" Intended to be an example of the versatility of a writer's notebook, (see Ralph Fletcher's *A Writer's Notebook* for more details) this book is absolutely charming. You get a peek inside a young writer's head and observe firsthand the many different ways a writer deals with a topic. It's clever, funny, and a guaranteed hit with students who know just how hard it is to get any privacy in this hectic world of ours!

Murray, Marjorie Dennis. ***Little Wolf and the Moon.*** Marshall Cavendish, 2002.
Hardcover: ISBN 0-7614-5100-5.
Each night Little Wolf sits in the mountain meadow pondering such questions as "How does the moon stay in the sky?" and "Where does the moon get its light?" A celebration of nature and the curiosity of the young, this story will generate lots of questions—some of which may not have ready answers.

Neuschwander, Cindy. ***Amanda Bean's Amazing Dream.*** Scholastic, 1998.
Hardcover (LB): ISBN 0-590-30012-1.
Amanda has a time problem: She isn't able to count fast enough to keep up with all the things that she needs to count. But then she discovers multiplication and her life takes a positive turn. A book to read and enjoy with those students who are fighting the idea of learning "tables."

Nolen, Jerdine. ***Raising Dragons.*** Silver Whistle, 1998. Hardcover: ISBN 0-15-201288-5.
There are some things you just know. But how to raise dragons? This unusual gift proves helpful to the whole family as they struggle through the real hardships of scratching a living from the ground. Huge, fanning wings and fire-breathing skills come to the rescue as nature creates difficult conditions on the farm and a little girl's ability to raise dragon hatchlings proves critical. A book to set young listeners' imaginations on fire. Also good for the trait of organization.

Nye, Naomi Shihab. ***Benito's Dream Bottle.*** Simon & Schuster, 1995.
Hardcover (LB): ISBN 0-02-768467-9.

Where do dreams come from? In this magical picture book, Benito's grandmother can't remember her dreams and young Benito searches his imagination for answers to his own dreams while exploring all sorts of delightful ways to help his grandmother remember. "Dreams are delivered by angels!" "Dreams ripen on trees!" "Dreams come out of elbows and toes!" A beautiful story to inspire ideas for stretching our imaginations through language.

Nye, Naomi Shihab. ***Sitti's Secrets.*** Bt Bound, 1999. Hardcover (LB): ISBN 0-613-05878-X.

A book about connections, this is a sensitive and thoughtful human story about the similarities we all share as we try to find our place in the world. Through the eyes of an Arabian American girl, we experience her bond with her Arabian grandmother and the rich culture that is a part of their life. I haven't found many books that do as fine a job with language barriers and very sensitive politics as this one. This piece would serve well as a model for building a sense of international community.

Oberman, Sheldon. ***The Always Prayer Shawl.*** Boyd Mills Press, 1994.
Hardcover (LB): ISBN 1-878093-22-3.

In a world of constant change, Adam, a young Jewish boy from Czarist Russia during the revolution, uses the treasured family prayer shawl to validate his Jewish traditions and give him the wisdom and strength to survive an extraordinary time in history. A deeply satisfying book, the story of the prayer shawl is richly told and thoughtful in its message. Watercolor illustrations are among my favorites, too, and so I find the pictures particularly well-suited to the topic. (Sydney Taylor Award winner: Association of Jewish Libraries, National Jewish Book Award winner from the Jewish Book Council; YA)

Okimoto, Jean Davies, and Aoki, Elaine M. ***The White Swan Express.***
Clarion Books, 2002. Hardcover (LB): ISBN 0-618-16453-7.

As I read this poignant story, I thought of my friends Barb and Terry who spoke to me of their excitement and of the long journey they made to collect their adopted Chinese daughters. This book captures that feeling accurately, and provides insights into the process of adoption that many of us may never experience. A wonderful eye opener. (YA)

Pinkwater, Daniel. ***The Picture of Morty and Ray.*** HarperCollins, 2003.
Hardcover (LB): ISBN 0-06-623786-6.

Morty and Ray decide to copy a classic movie *(The Picture of Dorian Gray)* and see if their painted portraits grow uglier as they commit unkind acts against their friends and schoolmates. But maybe their experiment is too successful, and friendships may be hard to come by once destroyed. A humorous look at a serious topic.

Polacco, Patricia. *The Graves Family.* Philomel Books, 2003.
Hardcover (LB): ISBN 0-399-24034-9.

The Graves family moves frequently from town to town because of their unusual ways. But Union City proves to be the exception as, in spite of their creepy habits, the Graves prove to be wonderful neighbors. A very funny story that carries an important message about the acceptance of differences. Also good for the trait of word choice.

Prather, Jo Beecher. *Mississippi Beau.* Eakin Press, 1995.
Paperback: ISBN 0-89015-961-0.

Ever wondered what treasures are housed in your state capitol building? Author Jo Prather did and began to research the beautiful capitol building in Jackson, Mississippi, in hopes that her piece would allow Mississippi school children a peek inside the historic site. With an eye toward the young reader, Prather creates the story of a squirrel, Beauregard Eisenhower Calvinlee Davis, to tell the story and reveal the treasures of this state building. What a wonderful model this is for children to learn how to research, use information, and reshape it into a piece that informs and tells a story at the same time!

Rathmann, Peggy. *Officer Buckle and Gloria.* G.P. Putnam, 1995.
Hardcover: ISBN 0-399-22616-8.

Officer Buckle's safety tip presentations are pretty dull until he is joined on stage by his new police dog Gloria. Unknown to Officer Buckle, Gloria has her own way of livening up his speeches and the audiences love it. And therein lies the problem: How can Officer Buckle keep making presentations when he knows that people have really come to see Gloria? A book with a clever ending, and you may even learn some useful safety tips, too.

Reynolds, Peter. *The Dot.* Candlewick Press, 2003. Hardcover (LB): ISBN 0-7636-1961-2.
The Dot is a book for all of us who do not aspire to great artistic skill. Vashti's teacher wisely tells her idea-blocked student, "Just make a mark and see where it takes you." The single, small mark leads Vashti on a voyage of discovery that she would never have imagined. This little tale is an excellent example of how getting down even the smallest, simplest idea can overcome the writer's block that occasionally visits all of us.

Ringgold, Faith. *Aunt Harriet's Underground Railroad in the Sky.* Bt Bound, 1999.
Hardcover (LB): ISBN 0-785-78483-7.

It's an art to capture so much rich history in such a short amount of space and words, but Faith Ringgold is one of the best in the field. She tackles an important subject, such as this one on the Underground Railroad, and teaches us about the role of the escaped slaves, the American Indians, the Abolitionists, and the Quakers. Her language is precise, honed, and powerful. Ringgold uses dialogue to allow us to understand this important part of U.S. history through the eyes of those most directly involved.

Robertson, M.P. *The Egg.* Phyllis Fogelman Books, 2001. Hardcover: ISBN 0-8037-2546-9.
George is not quite sure what will come from the huge egg he discovers in mom's chicken coop, but he knows that he has the responsibility to care for it whatever "it" turns out to be. And it turns out to be a dragon! George does his best to be a teacher and parent, but there is something missing from his young dragon's life—something only another dragon can provide. Will they be able to find it together? A gentle, beautifully illustrated tale of real friendship.

Robinson, Aminah Brenda Lynn. *A Street Called Home.* Harcourt Brace, 1997.
Hardcover: ISBN 0-15-201465-9.
After you read this uniquely formatted and expressive book you may know more about Mount Vernon Avenue than you do about your own street. At first glance, it is a fold-out book. Each page represents a person who lives on the street and their job or role. But then open the door … you walk in and find a delightful piece written in exquisite detail about the person. Then, stand the book on its side and it folds out, accordion style, into a display. An inspiring idea for students to look at and create their own "Street Called Home" or perhaps a book about the people at school. Every time I look at this book I see more—it's not only clever, but has vivid and descriptive detail on every page.

Rockwell, Anne F. *Welcome to Kindergarten.* Walker and Co., 2001.
Hardcover (LB): ISBN 0-8027-8746-0.
The idea of going to kindergarten becomes much more manageable for Tim as he examines the centers he will work at, and the desk he will use. A gentle introduction to the world of school aimed at calming the fears of youngsters entering the world of "big kids."

Rosen, Michael, Ed. *Home.* HarperCollins, 1992. Hardcover: ISBN 0-06-021788-X.
In this collection of 30 stories, poems, and illustrations, celebrated children's authors give a rich and diverse response to the question "What does home mean?" From grandma's kitchen table, to the mysteries of a dark spooky closet, from humorous to serious—the range of answers is complete.

Schaefer, Carole Lexa. *The Squiggle.* Bt Bound, 1999. Hardcover (LB): ISBN 0-613-18193-X.
Some things are not what they appear, and this wonderfully creative story is all about that. This piece, best suited for younger readers and writers, is a charming story of what happens to a piece of string once it is in the hands of a delightfully imaginative young Chinese girl.

Schroeder, Alan. *Ragtime Tumpie.* Bt Bound, 1999. Hardcover (LB): ISBN 0-785-71150-3.
Sepia-tinted watercolors and no-nonsense language recount the warm and understated story of how legendary dancer Josephine Baker, born into abject poverty in St. Louis, Missouri, discovers her own unique and remarkable talent. With the help of an encouraging mother, "Ragtime Tumpie" acquires the indomitable spirit that will carry her far from her St. Louis beginnings into worldwide fame. The author begins with a few simple facts, but embellishes them with believable characterizations and just enough detail to satisfy the reader's curiosity. An excellent example of how to tell a simple story well without getting bogged down in trivia and without telling too much.

Scillian, Devin. ***Cosmo's Moon.*** Sleeping Bear Press, 2003. Hardcover: ISBN 1-58536-123-2. Cosmo loves the moon so much that he wills it to stay with him night *and* day. But that has enormous repercussions for the rest of the world: The tides lose their way, dogs howl constantly, and Morning Glory never blooms. But most important for Cosmo, never saying goodbye to the moon also means never saying hello. A story that speaks to both the beauty of nature, and personal responsibility. Also good for the trait of presentation. (YA)

Shannon, George. ***Tomorrow's Alphabet.*** Bt Bound, 1999. Hardcover (LB): ISBN 0-613-18196-4. This splendid gift is from an insightful friend, Gaye Lantz, who knows a book that will inspire kids to write and think when she sees one! This unusual ABC book helps students develop their higher level thinking skills by playing with the alphabet, words, and connections—and the trick is, you have to do all that while thinking ahead to TOMORROW …. Students could be challenged to make up their own tomorrow's alphabet or even yesterday's alphabet. You could give them the tomorrow word from a specific content area like science or history and let them figure out the today or yesterday word. This book is rich with possibilities. My favorite: "U is for stranger—tomorrow's US."

Shoulders, Michael. ***Count on Us: A Tennessee Number Book.*** Sleeping Bear Press, 2003. Hardcover: ISBN 1-58536-131-3.

A companion series to its successful alphabet books, this Sleeping Bear Press offering takes us state by state through the numbers one to 100. To introduce us to his state of Tennessee, Michael Shoulders combines the number concept with fascinating information; we not only count 10 flickering fireflies, we also learn that they are not flies at all, but beetles. Look for your state's book.

Shoulders, Michael. ***V Is for Volunteer: A Tennessee Alphabet.*** Sleeping Bear Press, 2001. Hardcover: ISBN 1-58536-033-3.

One of a series that will eventually include all the states, *V Is for Volunteer* combines poetic descriptions and prose information in an alphabetic march through the important people, places, and events of Tennessee's history. Michael and award-winning illustrator Bruce Langton turn history into an exciting journey of discovery for young and not-so-young readers. And thank you, Michael, for your friendship and generosity on my visit to Tennessee. (YA)

Simon, Seymour. ***They Swim the Seas: The Mystery of Animal Migration.*** Raintree/Steck Vaughn, 1998. Hardcover (LB): ISBN 0-817-25765-9.

From tiny plankton to the giant gray whale, from the elevator ride of herring to the single-file march of the spiny lobster, Mr. Simon takes us on a fascinating journey of discovery and wonder in the world's oceans as he describes the migratory habits of creatures that inhabit the water world. This book will answer many questions, and raise as many more for young scientists seeking to understand the natural world.

Simon, Seymour. *They Walk the Earth.* Browndeer Press, 2000.
Hardcover (LB): ISBN 0-739-82196-2.

> Here is yet another extraordinarily informative book from this prolific writer. Follow the caribou of the tundra, the lemmings of Norway, and the elephants of the African grasslands as they travel hundreds of miles in their constant search for food and living space. Read, too, about humans who travel with their animals even today. Full of accurate detailed information, these are great books to get kids hooked on scientific inquiry.

Sis, Peter. *The Three Golden Keys.* Frances Foster Books, 1994. Hardcover: ISBN 0-385-47292-7.

> Blown off-course in a hot-air balloon, a man lands in his childhood hometown. But when he tries to enter the house of his birth he finds he needs three keys. So starts this adventure that takes us through a maze of Czech legends, always led by a lucky black cat, in search of the golden keys. Simply written and intricately illustrated, this is a complex journey of the imagination for older listeners. Also good for the trait of organization. (YA)

Steig, William. *When Everybody Wore a Hat.* Joanna Cotler Books, 2003.
Hardcover (LB): ISBN 0-06-009701-9.

> this is history in the first person. A recollection of a time almost 100 years ago is the foundation of this little book that is sure to get youngsters asking questions like "How did they live without TV?" So, why did everyone wear a hat? (YA)

Steptoe, John. *Mufaro's Beautiful Daughters.* William Morrow, 1987.
Hardcover (LB): ISBN 0-688-04046-2.

> Based on an old folktale, this is the story of two sisters who vie for the right to be chosen as wife to the king. The chosen one must be "the most worthy," but one of the sisters forgets this condition and sets out to make sure she is chosen. This subterfuge backfires, of course, and we are left with a powerful moral. Beautiful illustrations, many containing detail from Zimbabwe's architecture, enhance this story. Also good for the trait of presentation. (YA)

Thaler, Mike. *The School Bus Driver From the Black Lagoon.* Bt Bound, 1999.
Hardcover (LB): ISBN 0-613-17939-0.

> Another of the *Black Lagoon* series, this little book takes us on a flight of fancy of what bus driver T. Rex Fenderbender MIGHT be like if all our worst nightmares became reality. But, of course, they don't and we're left wishing that perhaps one or two of our fancies might be true. *(Principal From the Black Lagoon* and *Teacher From the Black Lagoon* also available.)

Van Allsburg, Chris. *Jumanji.* Houghton Mifflin, 1981. Hardcover: ISBN 0-395-30448-2.

> In a good fantasy, the line between real and imaginary is sometimes hard to pinpoint. When a board game comes to life, is the world really changing, or is the change only in the minds of the players? It's a fascinating question, deftly posed by a writer who clearly thrills in the mystical magic of make-believe. Like all Van Allsburg books, this one provides an excellent illustration of how to give fantasy real appeal by keeping one foot in reality.

Van Allsburg, Chris. ***Zathura.*** Houghton Mifflin, 2002. Hardcover: ISBN 0-618-25396-3.
Many of us remember the Jumanji game, where game pieces and moves became reality. In this story, the game is Zathura, and the location is space. Danny and his brother step into it unwittingly, and find themselves struggling for survival. Another super journey of the imagination for all ages of listeners. Also good for the trait of organization. (YA)

Weir, Bob. ***Panther Dream: A Story of the African Rainforest.*** Hyperion Press, 1991.
Hardcover (LB): ISBN 1-56282-075-3.
While hunting for food to feed his starving village, a young boy encounters a panther who teaches him how to conserve life in the rain forest. The information in this book is clear and accurate, but thanks to the picture book format, much more interesting and understandable than many textbooks on the same topic. Students relate to the main characters and their stories while internalizing contexts, facts, and subject material and applying it to their own and others' lives. Use to illustrate voice and word choice, too.

Wick, Walter. ***A Drop of Water: A Book of Science and Wonder.*** Scholastic, 1997.
Hardcover (LB): ISBN 0-590-22197-3.
Here's a great find! A book of science in picture book form, but heavy on content. This whole collection of unique photographs magnifies all the amazing states in which water can be observed —as ice, in rainbows, as steam, in frost, and in dew. Scientific processes such as evaporation, condensation, surface tension, and capillary attraction are explained in eloquent and simple text. This book is a magnificent blend of art and science—not to mention stand-out quality in expository writing.

Willis, Jeanne. ***Susan Laughs.*** Henry Holt, 2000. Hardcover (LB): ISBN 0-8050-6501-6.
This is a surprisingly fresh and unsentimental look at the normality of the life of a young girl with physical challenges. There is no way that Susan is going to let her wheelchair be an impediment to living life to the fullest, and you would never know a wheelchair was in the picture unless you turned to the last page. Bravo, Susan! Also good for the trait of sentence fluency.

Winter, Jonah. ***Frida.*** Arthur A. Levine Books, 2002. Hardcover: ISBN 0-590-20320-7.
Here is the story of the extraordinary courage of Mexican artist Frida Kahlo. Having suffered from polio and then injured in a bus crash as a youngster, Kahlo was in constant pain throughout her life. Working through the pain, she was able to create beautiful paintings, and she says it was those paintings that saved her life. An inspiring lesson for all of us, and particularly our daughters. Also good for the trait of sentence fluency. (The book is also available in Spanish.)

Woolf, Virginia. ***Nurse Lugton's Curtain.*** Gulliver Books, 2004.
Hardcover (LB): ISBN 0-15-205048-5.
This is one of Virginia Woolf's most enchanting stories. As Nurse Lugton dozes in her chair by the hearth, the drawing-room curtain she has been sewing lies motionless across her lap. But in the curtain's intricate pattern of wild animals, lakes, bridges, and towns, a wonderful and magical world slowly unfolds. This is another excellent book to use in response to the favorite object prompt, which might show students how to approach this topic in a personal, creative, and meaningful way.

We need to consider picture books as literature—not children's literature—but as literature.

—Thomas Newkirk, *Beyond Words: Picture Books for Older Readers and Writers*

Organization

Enticing lead
Strong transitions with easy-to-follow sequencing
Powerhouse conclusion

Abercrombie, Barbara. ***Charlie Anderson.*** Bt Bound, 1999. Hardcover (LB): ISBN 0-785-76383-X.
   At first glance, this is just a cute story about a cat. I love cats, so I liked it from the get go. However, the ending was magnificent, and I realized the author carefully foreshadowed what was to come; I just hadn't picked up on the clues. It's easy to do with picture books. They are deceptively simple on the surface. This piece, however, is a prime example of how important organization can be to enhance and highlight the ideas and theme. And the theme in this case is how families can be very happy and successful and share time with each other even when one family becomes two families or even more due to divorce, remarriage, and so forth. I think you'll find that *Charlie Anderson* is a book you won't want to be without no matter what the age of the students with whom you work.

Ahlberg, Janet, and Ahlberg, Allan. ***It Was a Dark and Stormy Night.*** Viking Press, 1994. Hardcover: ISBN 0-670-84620-1.
   Who says this is one of the most trite beginnings of all time? In this imaginative story, blood-thirsty brigands, pirates, parrots, and chocolate cake take you on an amazing journey where anything could happen on a dark and stormy night ….

Bang, Molly. ***Chattanooga Sludge.*** Gulliver Green Books (Harcourt Brace), 1996. Hardcover (LB): ISBN 0-15-2163-45-X.
   I've never seen a book formatted the way this one is. It will draw you into the story of Chattanooga Creek via the science, technology, and sheer willpower it took to save it from becoming an environmental disaster zone! From the first page (actually, the inside front cover), which takes you back through time, millions and millions of years ago, this piece moves through the story of the formation of the most significant rivers and land masses in the region with amazing speed and accuracy. A few pages in, you begin the story of Chattanooga Creek that unfolds not only in narrative form, but also with little rabbitlike characters on each page commenting on the most significant ideas as the story moves along. You'll learn so much as you read this book, and be delighted as you go. Molly Bang makes the world of environmental science accessible even to our earliest readers. For older readers, this piece is a real challenge—let them use this format to create their own research pieces. (YA)

Bang, Molly. ***The Grey Lady and the Strawberry Snatcher.*** Simon & Schuster, 1984.
Hardcover (LB): ISBN 0-02-7081-40-0.

Wordless picture books cause the reader to look for and build connections and transitions from one idea or picture to the next. In this beautifully illustrated story, the Grey Lady takes her basket of strawberries on a walk through the city while the Strawberry Snatcher is close on her heels, lurking in shadows and stalking her as she goes. This wordless allegory relies heavily on little visual details as it leads you through the fantastic and improbable. Readers find themselves poring over each picture to piece together a story of humor, suspense, and wonder. (Caldecott Honor Book)

Banyai, Istvan. ***Zoom*** and ***ReZoom.*** Viking Press, 1995.
Hardcovers: ISBN 0-670-85804-8 and 0-670-86392-0.

Both of these colorful and original wordless picture books illustrate a series of events with all kinds of interesting and unique people and places. The hook with these books is organization. Each picture either zooms in or out from the last one, gradually revealing a bigger and bigger context for the settings and people. A bit confused? That's not surprising since these books are 100 percent visual and defy words to do them justice. These are the books referenced in one of the teaching strategy lesson plans for organization …. Check 'em out. They're fascinatingly (good word choice, eh?) addictive! (YA)

Blake, Quentin. ***Clown.*** Henry Holt, 1996. Hardcover: ISBN 0-8050-4399-3.

Gotta love those wordless picture books for helping students make connections, see transitions, and look for sequencing. This one really caught my eye because it is by the illustrator most associated with Roald Dahl's works. Quentin Blake strikes out on his own here with the story of Clown, who starts in a garbage can and ends up with a perfectly content family.

Blos, Joan W. ***Old Henry.*** Mulberry Books (William Morrow), 1987.
Paperback: ISBN 0-688-09935-1.

Poor old Henry! The neighbors want him to clean, paint, and tidy up. But he'd rather smell the flowers, chat over coffee, and enjoy his birds. Finally, tired of being pestered by busybodies who won't let him be himself, Henry moves away. But—surprise! Henry and his nosy neighbors miss one another. He writes a heartfelt note to the mayor: Could he come back, but on his own terms? There this warm and wonderful little tale ends, inviting student writers to invent a conclusion to their own liking. Perhaps a letter from the mayor to Henry? Tenderly told in soft, subtle rhyme. Beautifully illustrated.

Briggs, Raymond. ***The Snowman.*** Random House, 1978. Hardcover: ISBN 0-394-83973-0.

An award-winning classic that's been called "a wordless wonder" *(The Christian Science Monitor),* this magical story of fantastic friendship tickles the imaginations of young and old alike. Wordless pictures offer students endless opportunities to generate personal text and to build transitions between events. What happens first? What happens next? How does the story end? Create an oral or written text to suit your own creative spirit. (American Library Association Notable Book, Boston Globe-Horn Book Award winner)

Burton, Virginia Lee. ***The Little House: Her Story.*** Houghton Mifflin, 1978.
Hardcover: ISBN 0-395-18156-9.

    This enduring tale of how the world surrounding a little house changes is just perfect for illustrating the use of time as an organizer for narrative writing. So much happens in this story of little house spirit vs. big city blight and smog—yet the text unfolds simply, always focusing on just what's important. If you haven't read Burton's story in a while, rediscover this charming old friend.

Christelow, Eileen. ***What Do Authors Do?*** Clarion Books (Houghton Mifflin), 1995.
Hardcover (LB): ISBN 0-395-71124-X.

    The whole story of how authors get an idea, suffer the indignities of rejections, finally get the contract to be published, and then go through the entire editing/publishing process is chronicled in this delightful cartoon text. As a reader, you follow two parallel stories from beginning to end. The subtext explores the "mysteries" of the writing process from draft to draft. This is a great book to show students where ideas come from, how to fine-tune them, and how to share them with others. It's honest, clever, and quite funny. But the organization is what struck me. Every step, starting with the first thinking about the topic through publishing, is documented and set forth in a systematic and believable way. What a great treatment of such an interesting idea!

dePaola, Tomie. ***The Legend of the Bluebonnet: An Old Tale of Texas.*** Putnam, 1983.
Paperback: ISBN 0-399-20937-9.

    The bluebonnet, or lupine, is the state flower of Texas. To the Commanche people, it also represents the legendary symbol of the Great Spirits' forgiveness and compassion for the people of the plains. According to the legend, She-Who-Is-Alone, a solitary, brave, and spiritual member of her nation, sacrifices what is most precious to her to free her people from the plague and torment of a long drought. When the rains come, the plains are covered in beautiful blue flowers, a sign that the Great Spirits will once again care for and protect the plains people. Tomie dePaola's unique illustrations bring a gentle grace to this tale of unselfish love. An outstanding example of strong organization structured around events that matter. (YA)

Doubilet, Anne. ***Under the Sea From A to Z.*** Crown, 1991. Hardcover: ISBN 0-517-57836-0.

    A useful organizational structure for reports and presenting information is the A–Z alphabet book. This lavishly illustrated book on sea animals makes a good place to begin. There are literally hundreds of new alphabet books on every topic imaginable now available in the picture book section of bookstores. Collect a variety to show students that creativity is an important part of making this format successful.

Drake, John W. ***Just Another Day.*** Little Turtle Press, 1995.
Hardcover: ISBN 0-9633574-1-7.

    Definitely for the left-brained person, this text is a desktop publisher's dream. Once you begin to connect with the organization of this piece, then the main idea begins to reveal itself. *Just Another Day* is a journey—it's an adventure. It also has an important message for those of us who might (occasionally) fall into the drudgery of the daily grind.

Duke, Kate. ***Aunt Isabel Tells a Good One.*** Bt Bound, 1999.
Hardcover (LB): ISBN 0-785-76457-7.

    Here's a story within a story. A great book to use to teach children about the elements that make a piece work: a heroine, a hero, energy and pizzazz, a little love interest, and even a bad guy or two. All the ingredients are contained between two covers. This piece, though probably best suited for primary and elementary readers, is enchanting and one that participants at workshops pick up and exclaim, "Oh, I love this book. My kids read it over and over again."

Dyer, Jane. ***Little Brown Bear Won't Go to School.*** Little Brown & Co., 2003.
Hardcover: ISBN 0-316-19685-1.

    Little Brown Bear decides school is not for him, so he sets off to find a job. But little bears with few skills can find the working world pretty tough, so the games and learning activities of the classroom become a much more attractive proposition.

Evans, Richard Paul. ***The Dance.*** Simon & Schuster, 1999. Hardcover: ISBN 0-689-82351-7.

    A beautiful account of a father's love and a daughter's devotion is guaranteed to bring a lump to your throat, as is the poignant story of the illustrations that bring this book to life. Students will easily follow the transitions in the girl's life from child to woman, and connect with the constant cycle of life. (YA)

Feiffer, Jules. ***Meanwhile ...*** HarperCollins, 1997. Hardcover (LB): 0-06-205156-3.

    Want to emphasize the importance of good transitions in student-generated text? Here is the perfect piece to share! In this fanciful, clever, and delightful story, Raymond learns the power of the term "meanwhile" as he literally lives adventure to adventure to adventure.

Fletcher, Ralph. ***Twilight Comes Twice.*** Clarion Books (Houghton Mifflin), 1997.
Hardcover (LB): ISBN 0-395-84826-1.

    What do you think of when you think of twilight? Dusk? Dawn? Both? In Ralph Fletcher's first outing as a picture book author (with many more to come, I hope!) he has captured the essence of these two special times of the day with his own remarkable free-verse poetry:

      "Twice each day
      a crack opens
      between night and day.
      Twice twilight
      slips through that crack."

The words and their images make this a thoughtful and engaging piece of writing, but even more interesting to those of us trying to use text like this to help students create their own original works, is Fletcher's use of organization. This piece is organized to chronicle the moments from dusk to dawn—not the other way around which would have been a traditional approach to the topic. I like that; it makes me stop and think about how many other ideas could be organized differently in text to help the ideas stand out more clearly. Beautiful word choice, gentle phrasing—a piece that you'll want to read over and over again.

Fox, Mem. ***Tough Boris.*** Harcourt Brace, 1994. Hardcover (LB): ISBN 0-15-289612-0.
What is it about pirates that holds such universal fascination for children? From the first line, I have seen kids sit motionless, totally enrapt in this piece and delighting in the repeating refrains that unfold throughout it. They chime in even before you tell them to—it's just natural! We learn a bit about labels, too. Though most kids think of pirates as tough, rough, and mean, this book shows a kinder, gentler side. And if that's true about pirates, maybe it is true about other mean people in their lives?

Gaiman, Neil. ***The Day I Swapped My Dad for Two Goldfish.*** White Wolf, 1997.
Hardcover (LB): ISBN 0-060-58702-4.
I guarantee, positively, absolutely, that you won't find another book quite like this one. The story is funny and insightful, the kind you absolutely can't put down once you start. But the formatting is what really grabs your attention. Told almost exclusively through dialogue, the reader gets a chance to experience firsthand the relationship between this brother and sister and how they, in turn, relate differently to their parents. What WOULD you trade your dad for? A transformer robot? A punching bag? Some baseball cards? Naw, a dad is worth a lot more than that! How about a goldfish in its own bowl? Now you're talking …. The characters are real and alive—just about as honest a portrait of kids as you can sandwich between two covers. Here's a little glimpse into the main character's perspective on life: "Some people have great ideas maybe once or twice in their life, and then they discover electricity, or fire or outer space or something. I mean, the kind of brilliant ideas that change the whole world. Some people never have them at all. I get them two or three times a week."

Gantos, Jack. ***Rotten Ralph.*** Houghton Mifflin, 1976. Hardcover (LB): ISBN 0-395-24276-2.
Purposeful sentence beginnings (Then, Next, The following day, After a while, etc.) hook ideas together in ways that make reading easier and stories more understandable. This technique is exceptionally well-illustrated in *Rotten Ralph.* But you don't have to read it just for the great transitions! My, no! The pictures are hilarious. And Ralph's incorrigible rottenness is a perfect complement to owner Sarah's unflagging loyalty and affection. A favorite among cat lovers (and nonlovers) and humor-loving people in general. (Great for teaching voice, too!)

Gerrard, Roy. ***The Favershams.*** Farrar, Straus and Giroux, 1983. Hardcover: ISBN 0-374-32292-9.
A tidy tale told in delightful rhyme makes this book fine for teaching sentence fluency as well. A "narrative sequence, recounting the exemplary, yet somehow otherworldly, lives of a Victorian officer and gentleman and his wife, *The Favershams* conveys an almost novelistic sense of the beauty, strangeness, and grandeur of everyday life in the years 1851–1914." —*Washington Post.* (Award winner for graphics and illustrations)

Goode, Diane. ***Tiger Trouble.*** Blue Sky Press, 2001. Hardcover (LB): ISBN 0-439-20866-1.
Jack and his pet tiger, Lily, have an idyllic life until Mr. Mud and his cat-hating bulldog Fifi take over the apartment building. Lily has to go. But events take their own course to change the minds of the newcomers, and give Lily a welcome reprieve. So, burglars beware!

Hall, Donald. *I Am the Dog, I Am the Cat.* Dial Books, 1994.
Hardcover (LB): ISBN 0-8037-1505-6.

> This is just the perfect book to inspire writers to try a different organizational structure. Each page of this clever and deliciously funny book is either from the dog's or the cat's point of view—each one right after the other. And boy, are they different. Anyone who has ever owned either or both of these animals as pets will enjoy the subtle yet significant differences in the way the animals act and react to each other, their environment, and humans. And the pictures are a perfect match to the text.

Hartman, Bob. *The Wolf Who Cried Boy.* Putnam's Sons, 2002.
Hardcover (LB): ISBN 0-399-23578-7.

> In a twist on the familiar cautionary tale, it is Little Wolf who decides to avoid eating lamburgers and three-pig salad by crying "Boy" and sending his parents on wild boy chases. Eventually, of course, his parents get wise to the game, so that when a Boy Scout troop really does appear in the woods, Little Wolf can get no help in catching one of the plump little scouts. Wonderfully colorful illustrations by Tim Raglin add to the excitement of the story.

Hest, Amy. *How To Get Famous in Brooklyn.* Simon & Schuster, 1995.
Hardcover (LB): ISBN 0-689-80293-5.

> How would you get famous in Brooklyn—or in any corner of the world, for that matter? Why, by writing, of course. Find out how to keep a journal, and fill it with interesting observations about the world that makes up your corner of the universe. Janie takes us on an observational tour of New York, showing us along the way that the tiniest details make the stuff of good stories. A fine prelude to any observational exercise, from a nature walk to a museum visit. Helps students see the value of paying attention to the little unobtrusive details that the best writers just never seem to miss.

Hoberman, Mary Ann. *The Seven Silly Eaters.* Gulliver Books, 1997.
Hardcover (LB): ISBN 0-15-200096-8.

> Here's a delightful romp through the ever-growing and complicated life of a family with seven children, all of whom are very picky eaters. Mom and dad are about the best-natured sorts in town, but there comes a time when even mom can't take it any more and has a complete and total breakdown. The kids come to the rescue, however, and all is well at the end. I love the way this piece builds, child by child in sequence, then crashes and pulls itself all together again by the conclusion. This would make a great piece to analyze for the elements of a successful story.

Jenkins, Steve. *Big & Little.* Houghton Mifflin, 1996. Hardcover (LB): ISBN 0-395-72664-6.

> One of the processes used to help students understand the trait of organization is comparison and contrast with sizes. This book (primarily suited for younger writers) is a collection of animals from all over the world, organized and shared in picture and text by size. It has lots of interesting little facts, too. For example, did you know that the capybara is the world's largest rodent and weighs as much as 1,000 mice? No? Well, I didn't either. Illustrated with stunning cut-paper collages, here is a chance to explore BIG & little all over the world.

Kramer, Stephen P. *How To Think Like a Scientist.* HarperCollins, 1987.
Hardcover (LB): ISBN 0-690-04565-4.

"Suppose you were riding your bicycle along a country road late one afternoon. Suppose you found a snake that had been killed by a car, but not too badly squashed. Suppose you scooped it into an empty plastic bag and tied the top of the bag in a tight knot. Suppose you put that bag into another plastic bag and sealed it tightly, too. And suppose you found a nice spot way in the back of the freezer where you could keep the snake awhile, a place where your mother would never find it. ... Well, with that snake and what you know about the scientific method, you could answer the question about dead snakes, tree branches, and rain all by yourself." Thus ends Steve Kramer's enlightening and student-friendly text on thinking scientifically. Through this extended picture book, students learn to set up hypotheses, work with control and experimental groups, record observations accurately, interpret results, and avoid misinformation—all in the context of everyday questions students themselves find interesting. Charmingly illustrated, beautifully organized, using the technique of posing and answering your own questions. Excellent for both ideas and voice, too.

Macaulay, David. *Black and White.* Houghton Mifflin, 1990.
Hardcover (LB): ISBN 0-395-52151-3.

"Warning: This book appears to contain a number of stories that do not necessarily occur at the same time. But it may contain only one story. Then again, there may be four stories. Or four parts of a story. Careful inspection of both words and pictures is recommended." One of the great illustrators of our time, David Macaulay invites readers to puzzle out the organization and therefore the story of this book. It's very intriguing and bound to create a lively discussion. (Caldecott Award winner)

Mann, Pamela. *The Frog Princess?* Gareth Stevens, 1995.
Hardcover (LB): ISBN 0-8368-1352-9.

Talk about your surprise endings. *The Frog Princess?* is an absolute MUST for any classroom that really values reading and writing. Just when you think you've heard this story before, talented Pamela Mann delivers a punch line with implications for discussion about censorship, surprise endings, and stereotypes. I like to use this piece as a shared reading so the students listening get the full impact of the twist at the end, but you use it however you want—just use it. It's a winner for sure!

Mathers, Petra. *Kisses From Rosa.* Knopf, 1995. Hardcover (LB): ISBN 0-679-92686-0.

Being separated from your mother can be immensely traumatic for a child, even if the reason is a good one. In this lovely piece, Rosa's mother is very ill, so Rosa is sent to stay with Aunt Mookie at the farm. Although Rosa is terribly homesick and misses her mother dreadfully, she becomes fascinated with the farm's activities ... like berry picking with old Mrs. Schmidt and visiting the cows with Cousin Birgit, and falling for Waldi, "the best dog in the whole wide world." Rosa sends kiss-filled letters to her mother brimming with love and encouragement. This is a heart-warming story based on the author's own experience.

McBratney, Sam. ***I'll Always Be Your Friend.*** HarperCollins, 2001.
Hardcover: ISBN 0-06-029485-X.

    Having to stop playing and head home for the night is hard on youngsters, and it is no easier on a little fox. So instead of going home with Mom he heads out on his own, only to find that shadows and noises are much scarier when she is not around. A lesson for young listeners in when to call it a day, and in a mother's patience. Also good for the trait of ideas.

Munsch, Robert. ***Aaron's Hair.*** Cartwheel Books, 2000. Hardcover: ISBN 0-439-19258-7.

    In the ultimate "bad hair day" book, Aaron learns the lesson of letting his hair get so long that it becomes unmanageable, and in fact it takes on a life of its own. Join him in his chase through town to retrieve the runaway hair and get it back where it belongs, maybe.

Noble, Trinka Hakes. ***Meanwhile, Back at the Ranch.*** Bt Bound, 1999.
Hardcover (LB): ISBN: 0-833-59283-1.

    Rancher Hicks lives a very quiet life—nothing much ever happens. He goes into town and nothing much ever happens there, either. However, while he's in town, his wife Elna has more and more exciting experiences with each successive page. This whole delightful story is organized by the phrase "Meanwhile, back at the ranch," or "Meanwhile, back at Sleepy Gulch," as Rancher Hicks's day gets progressively more boring and Elna's gets wilder and wilder. This picture book would be a terrific model of how to organize using a repetitive phrase to move the reader through the text. Lively and fun—very imaginative. (Use for ideas, too.)

O'Malley, Kevin. ***Herbert Fieldmouse, Secret Agent.*** Mondo Publishing, 2003.
Hardcover: ISBN 1-593-36042-8.

    Employing the staccato style of 1950s detective movies, this story carries you on a fast-paced adventure interspersed with clever tongue-in-cheek humor that will hold listeners' attention right up to the last clever twist. Written in the first person, it is a good example of how to authentically capture voice in a story. Also good for the traits of voice and sentence fluency.

Paul, Ann Whitford. ***The Seasons Sewn: A Year in Patchwork.***
Browndeer Press, Harcourt Brace, 1996. Hardcover (LB): ISBN 0-15-276918-8.

    It is impossible for us to truly imagine what life was like on a farm more than 100 years ago, but this fine work is a good start. Organized by quilt pattern, a sense of unity, harmony, and community unfold to show us a great deal of 19th century life. With its carefully illustrated and finely detailed quilt designs, readers of all ages will savor this wonderful book. I'm going to give a copy to my mom for Christmas—she's a quilter and will truly appreciate the detail and thoughtful treatment of the craft in this work.

Paulsen, Gary. ***The Tortilla Factory.*** Harcourt Brace, 1995. Hardcover (LB): ISBN 0-15-292876-6.

    Using the cycle of life as the organizational structure, Gary Paulsen once again amazes us with his use of eloquent and simple everyday words. He is the master at writing prose so well that it reads like poetry—attention to every syllable, sound, and nuance of the language is always present. You'll love Ruth Paulsen's paintings that accompany this text—they are rich, earthy, and textured for perfect harmony.

Pelés, Les Chats. *Long Live Music.* Creative Editions (Harcourt Brace), 1996.
Hardcover (LB): ISBN 0-15-201310-5.
> Now here's a piece to inspire young writers through creative use of text and formatting. Walk/run through this whimsical journey of Phil and his dog, Pippo, as Silence the Giant takes all the musical instruments away. Follow the story upside down, in, and around through twists and turns—the book must be held in all different directions to read the text and keep the story moving. As a wonderful bonus, the reader also gets a short history of different musical instruments and music itself as the story unfolds.

Polacco, Patricia. *My Ol' Man.* Philomel Books, 1995. Hardcover (LB): ISBN 0-399-22822-5.
> So many things about this book are worth talking about, but I am particularly struck by its powerful opening and the way the context of the story is framed in two short sentences. The piece moves with masterful pacing and perfectly constructed phrasing. And the story itself is magical and unique. I'd use this piece with Byrd Baylor's *The Rock.* Both books use rocks as the mysterious center for imagination and ideas.

Rohmann, Eric. *My Friend Rabbit.* Roaring Brook Press, 1999.
Hardcover (LB): ISBN 0-7613-2420-8.
> When mouse's new airplane gets stuck in a tree, his friend rabbit has the solution. Or does he? Maybe the solution will create a bigger problem than they had in the first place. A cautionary tale, told mostly through the beautiful relief-print illustrations.

Ryan, Pam Muñoz. *The Flag We Love.* Charlesbridge, 1996. Hardcover: ISBN 0-88106-845-4.
> The Fourth of July usually falls outside the school calendar, so to remind us of all that is American about this day, this poetic piece will be a good addition to your books honoring America's finest traditions and heritage. There are little tidbits of historical reference to the flag tucked in among descriptions of commonly held traditions related to this symbol. In an interesting organizational format, the piece is written in verse, but on each page are several starred facts that enhance our understanding and appreciation of the American flag.

Schories, Pat. *Mouse Around.* Farrar, Straus and Giroux, 1991. Hardcover: ISBN 0-374-35080-9.
> Follow the adventures of an adorable little mouse who finds himself out in the world struggling to make his way safely home to mother, brothers, and sisters. Using realistic, detailed pictures, this wordless picture book tells its story by emphasizing sequence and transitions. Good practice for writers of any age working with organization strategies!

Van Allsburg, Chris. *The Mysteries of Harris Burdick.* Houghton Mifflin, 1984.
Hardcover (LB): ISBN 0-395-35393-9.
> "When Chris Van Allsburg was invited to the home of Peter Wenders, he discovered 14 drawings that were, like pieces of a picture puzzle, clues to larger pictures. But the puzzles, the mysteries, presented by these drawings, are not what we are used to. They are not solved for us, as in the final pages of a book or a film's last reel. The solutions to these mysteries lie in a place at once close at hand, yet far more remote. They lie in our imagination." Looking for a good open-ended way to spark imagination and prompt writing? Try using these pictures, which also come in poster-sized prints available from the publisher. (YA)

Van Allsburg, Chris. ***Two Bad Ants.*** Houghton Mifflin, 1988.
Hardcover (LB): ISBN 0-395-48668-8.
> If ever there was a model for good organization, it is an ant colony! In this inventive and highly creative story, the queen of the ant colony declares that a marvelous crystal which has been discovered in a faraway place, is the most delicious substance she has ever eaten. The other ants set out to bring it back to the queen, but not without a few twists and turns in between. Chris Van Allsburg is a master at creating strange yet satisfying tales of ordinary things played out with a twist. Here is a great piece to share with students as they follow the logic of the ant colony's quest and the inevitable consequences.

Viorst, Judith. ***Alexander and the Terrible, Horrible, No Good, Very Bad Day.*** Atheneum, 1972.
Hardcover (LB): ISBN 0-689-30072-7.
> Alexander knew it was going to be a terrible day when he woke up with gum in his hair. And it got worse …. As this classic story unfolds, each event appears to make the day even worse than before. Copy this story and insert students' own versions of what would make the worst day ever! (For Spanish version, see Page 71.)

Walsh, Ellen Stoll. ***Jack's Tale.*** Harcourt Brace, 1997. Hardcover (LB): ISBN 0-15-200323-1.
> Perfect to introduce the idea of the elements of story to our youngest readers and writers, *Jack's Tale* begins at the beginning, shows how to develop an "interesting middle" and end, of course, "happily ever after." Clever, original, and charming, this little piece has all the elements of a strong narrative along with just a dash of excitement and suspense.

Wiesner, David. ***Tuesday.*** Bt Bound, 1999. Hardcover (LB): ISBN 0-613-03614-X.
> In this inventive and clever book, David Wiesner uses the organizational structure of one day, Tuesday, to create a whole series of bizarre and improbable incidents. The book jacket describes it best: "The events recorded here are verified by an undisclosed source to have happened somewhere, U.S.A., on Tuesday. All those in doubt are reminded that there is always another TUESDAY."

Wiesner, David. ***June 29, 1999.*** Clarion Books (Houghton Mifflin), 1992.
Hardcover (LB): ISBN 0-395-59762-5.
> Like Wiesner's other books, this one is alive with imagination. "June 29, 1999, is a date no one will forget, particularly Holly Evans of Ho-Ho-Kus, New Jersey. Holly had great expectations for her science project when she sent seedlings aloft into the ionosphere, but she never imagined results that would be thereto unprecedented in scale. Holly can't believe that she is responsible for the fantastic events of June 29, 1999—and it may be just possible that she is right!"

Williams, Vera B. *A Chair for My Mother.* Greenwillow Books (William Morrow), 1982. Hardcover (LB): ISBN 0-688-00915-8.

Among the simplest organizational structures for beginning storytellers is to set up a problem and solve it. This story does just that. A loving family has lost their home to fire. Mom is a waitress, on her feet all day, exhausted when she returns to their tiny, barren apartment. Together, mother, daughter, and granddaughter save mom's tips in a jar and watch their treasure grow till they have enough to buy her a special chair as bright and glowing as the love they feel for her. This is a story of courage, caring, and tenderness told in direct, unsentimental language that reveals characters' feelings through their actions. A book to make you smile inside.

Winter, Jeanette. *Josefina.* Harcourt Brace, 1996. Hardcover (LB): ISBN 0-15-201091-2.

Josefina is an artist and this is her story. The setting is Ocotlan, Mexico, where young Josefina learns to work the clay and make one figure, then two, and more and more until she progressively adds to her beautifully constructed clay house each of the pieces that make it whole. Gracious in its language, poetic in phrasing, *Josefina* is a piece that should delight young readers with its patterns and repeating sequences.

Zemach, Margot. *It Could Always Be Worse.* Bt Bound, 1999. Hardcover (LB): ISBN 0-833-50706-0.

A poor, unfortunate man thinks his life is in terrible shape because his home is overcrowded and everyone fights all the time. The man consults his rabbi, who instructs him to bring a succession of farm animals into his home—making each day worse and worse—until finally, the man gets rid of all the farm animals and thinks life is once again good and peaceful. The structure of this book is a good one for students to copy when organizing their own stories. (Caldecott Honor Book)

Zolotow, Charlotte. *The Old Dog.* HarperCollins, 1995. Hardcover (LB): ISBN 0-06-02412-7.

Here's a book that is perfectly suited to expand the idea of voice, simple and true and coming from the heart. I love this piece by acclaimed author Charlotte Zolotow, but somehow, I'd like to see it end one page sooner. If you have a copy of this book, ask your students what they think. Does the ending work the way it is? Or does the author go one step too far?

The texts children write are more likely to resemble the texts of picture books than longer books composed of extended chapters. Whatever their reading preferences they [children older than second grade] will need the picture books as models for their writing.
—Thomas Newkirk, *Beyond Words: Picture Books for Older Readers and Writers*

Voice

Lively engagement and commitment
Audience and purpose for writing are in sync
The writer enjoyed it and hopes you will, too

Abeel, Samantha. ***Reach for the Moon.*** Pfeifer-Hamilton, 1994. Hardcover: ISBN 1-57025-013-8.
This is a moving collection of short writings and poems by a 12-year-old learning disabled student struggling to find her voice. Samantha, a remarkably gifted writer for whom math is a nightmare, teaches us an important lesson about labeling. Her riveting story shows how a teacher's insightful support can literally turn a confusing and frightening world of learning into one filled with promise and possibility. Don't miss the introduction—it will inspire and affirm.

Angelou, Maya. ***Life Doesn't Frighten Me.*** Stewart, Tabori, & Chang, 1996.
Hardcover: ISBN 1-55670-288-4.
Here is one of the most powerful picture books of all time! Through Angelou's brave and defiant poem, this glorious book challenges each of us to examine the dark and scary images hidden deep inside ourselves. The poem unfolds through a series of contrasting drawings and ideas—from big ghosts in a cloud to panthers and strangers in the dark. Readers are urged to summon their inner strength, to examine and dispel frightening thoughts, and to find faith in themselves.

Boyd, Candy Dawson. ***Daddy, Daddy, Be There.*** Bt Bound, 1999.
Hardcover (LB): ISBN 0-613-11463-9.
With its repeating refrain, "Daddy, Daddy, be there," echoing through the pages, this simple, yet poignant piece pulls at every parent's heart. It reminds us that children need unconditional and forever love—as much for the everyday business of living as for the events that mark our lives. I like this book so much because it is real; it shows families in conflict as well as in harmony. But always, it calls to us to hold out our hands and hearts to our children because they are desperate for the sense of belonging that only a family can bring. (Thank you, Janet Malek, for this wonderful gift.)

Bradby, Marie. ***More Than Anything Else.*** Orchard Books, 1995. Hardcover: ISBN 0-531-08764-6.
More Than Anything Else, young Booker T. Washington wants to learn to read, only the reader of this eloquent and moving book doesn't know the main character is Booker T. Washington until the end, which makes the voice even more powerful and underscores the theme of this book with additional import. On the surface, it is an affirming tribute to the power that language brings to any person's life; but the book can be read as a reminder that language is power and this book is a dramatic example of what happens when one group of people are denied access to that power.

Bruchac, Joseph. *Between Earth & Sky: Legends of Native American Sacred Places.* Bt Bound, 1999. Hardcover (LB): ISBN 0-613-15731-1.

There are many stories about sacred places from coast to coast, east to west. This majestic picture book celebrates 10 stories that help us understand the land around us—from mountains to oceans, prairies to canyons. It teaches us how to look at the beauty of our world through eyes that seek balance and harmony. I think my favorite is the Hopi legend that explains why we have canyons and craters on the earth. It seems that people once came from another world beneath this one. And before that, people came from another world. Each time things started to go wrong in these worlds (people getting jealous, fighting each other, forgetting to respect the sacred) the coyote stole the water monster's child. When the water monster got his child back, he retaliated by flooding the world. Each time this happened, people had to climb to higher places to be safe. The canyons are part of our world today to remind us of why and how we lost the hearts of some of our lands.

Bunting, Eve. *December.* Harcourt Brace, 1997. Hardcover (LB): ISBN 0-15-201434-9.

In this sensitive and poignant Christmas story, young Simon has a magical experience that changes how he thinks of this special day for the rest of his life. Through the richly illustrated text, we explore the generosity of Simon's mother as she invites a homeless woman into their house for Christmas Eve and Simon's reaction to sharing this time with a stranger. Even in this short amount of text, the reader watches a character develop, mature, and reflect. Eve Bunting's style is one that invites introspection; this latest piece is another jewel in her crown.

Bunting, Eve. *Fly Away Home.* Clarion Books (Houghton Mifflin), 1991. Hardcover (LB): ISBN 0-395-55962-6.

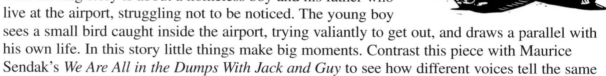

This moving story is about a homeless boy and his father who live at the airport, struggling not to be noticed. The young boy sees a small bird caught inside the airport, trying valiantly to get out, and draws a parallel with his own life. In this story little things make big moments. Contrast this piece with Maurice Sendak's *We Are All in the Dumps With Jack and Guy* to see how different voices tell the same tragic stories.

Bunting, Eve. *Going Home.* Joanna Cotler Books (HarperCollins), 1996. Hardcover (LB): ISBN 0-06-026297-4.

There is a special bond between Eve Bunting and her readers. She writes about a variety of topics, but each one reaches out and touches your heart in such a gentle and personal way, you feel as though the story was written just for you. In this fine, fine piece, a family born in Mexico now lives and works in the United States. "'We are going home, Carlos,' Mama says, hugging me. She sparkles with excitement. 'Home is here,' she says. But it is there, too. She and Papa are happy. My sisters and I are not so sure. Mexico is not our home." So begins a Christmas vacation to La Perla to remember. The journey symbolizes the family's struggle to maintain their past, honor their culture, and yet provide opportunities for a new life for the children. This is a remarkable book, able to weave together in a very short space so much that is important for all of us to think about as we teach and learn with our students from all over the world.

Bunting, Eve. ***The Memory String.*** Clarion Books (Houghton Mifflin), 2000.
Hardcover (LB): ISBN 0-395-86146-2.
> Laura's memory string holds buttons that represent events in her family's history—a button
> from great aunt's quilting dress, one from great grandmother's first grown-up dress, even one
> from dad's army shirt in the Gulf War. But the saddest, and most important is the button from
> her mom's nightdress that she was wearing when she died. When the string is accidentally bro-
> ken and the buttons scattered, it falls to Laura's stepmother to find the last elusive button, and in
> so doing begin the process of healing and connection with Laura that the youngster so desper-
> ately needs. A poignant story of loss and grieving that many youngsters will find familiar. (YA)

Bunting, Eve. ***The Wall.*** Clarion Books (Houghton Mifflin), 1990.
Hardcover (LB): ISBN 0-395-51588-2.
> A father and his young son visit the Vietnam Memorial to find the name of the grandfather the
> boy never knew. It's a tale that never flinches from the heartache and sadness of the situation,
> but gains spirit from the sense of pride and honor father and son find together. An excellent text
> for illustrating the integrity and power of voice in writing that is not derived from humor.

Coerr, Eleanor. ***Sadako.*** Putnam, 1993. Hardcover (LB): ISBN 0-399-21771-1.
> Caldecott medalist Ed Young's beautiful pastel illustrations bring to life the classic story of
> Sadako and her brave struggle against the leukemia she develops at age 12, 10 years after the
> atom bomb was dropped on Hiroshima. The Japanese legend holds that if a person who is ill
> makes a thousand paper cranes, the gods will grant that person's wish to be well again. This
> story is about the courage and strength of Sadako and the lessons of our own history. (Editor's
> Choice, Gold Award; YA)

Coleman, Evelyn. ***White Socks Only.*** Albert Whitman, 1996.
Hardcover (LB): ISBN 0-8075-8955-1.
> This is a magical story inspired by the author's personal memories of things she could not do
> and places she could not go because of her skin color. It is written with integrity and courage.
> However, it is also a celebration of African American tradition and culture that leaves the reader
> moved and hopeful.

Curry, Barbara K. ***Sweet Words So Brave.*** Zino Press, 1996. Hardcover: ISBN 1-55933-179-8.
> Middle and high school-aged students will appreciate the quality of this literature collection
> honoring the traditions of African American writers. From Phyllis Wheatley, the first published
> African American poet, to Toni Morrison, the first African American to win the Nobel Prize for
> literature, this vibrantly illustrated picture book will inspire and teach. (YA)

Dahl, Roald. ***The Twits.*** Knopf, 2002. Hardcover: ISBN 0-375-82242-9.
> The Twits are hardly the ideal married couple. Mrs. Twit puts worms in Mr. Twit's spaghetti—
> until he complains it's a little more chewy than his favorite brand. He retaliates by adding just a
> smidgen of wood to her walking cane each day, telling her she suffers from the dreaded shrinks
> and will probably have to be stretched—painful though that might be. These unsavory, unpleas-
> ant people torment both each other and their pet monkeys till the ingenious Muggle-Wumps find
> a way to outdo their nasty prankster-caretakers. Great fun, with the ribald, to-the-point humor
> for which Roald Dahl is famous.

Darrow, Sharon. ***Through the Tempests Dark and Wild: A Story of Mary Shelley.*** Candlewick Press, 2003. Hardcover (LB): ISBN 0-7636-0835-1.

Creator of Frankenstein, Mary Shelley was a weaver of scary tales from her youth. But it was not until she left the congestion of London to live with family friends in a small Scottish town that she was able to find the courage to explore her author's "voice." And it is this portion of her life that Sharon Darrow weaves into a fascinating story within a story. Accompanied by the atmospheric illustrations of Angela Barrett, this book will capture the imagination of older readers. (YA)

Fanelli, Sarah. ***Dear Diary.*** Candlewick Press, 2000. Hardcover: ISBN 0-7636-0965-X.

What starts as a diary entry of Lucy's day at school turns into a view of the world from the perspective of some of the characters that live around her; from the chair that got knocked over in class, to the ladybug who finally finds her mate. A cleverly constructed tale that shows how voice can change with character.

Fox, Mem. ***Whoever You Are.*** Harcourt Brace, 1997. Hardcover (LB): ISBN 0-15-200787-3.

"Little one, whoever you are, there are little ones just like you all over the world." So begins this magical book that reminds us that we may look different, live in different places, and go to different schools, but we all cry the same, bleed the same, and feel pain the same. The way this piece is written could easily make it a read-aloud with different students assigned to individual lines and parts. The refrain adds a sense of roundness and texture, but most important of all is the common bond of humanity that Mem Fox so masterfully weaves into all her pieces. This one in particular reminds us all to celebrate our differences and our similarities for we have much to learn from one another.

Ganeri, Anita. ***Out of the Ark: Stories From the World's Religions.*** Harcourt Brace, 1996. Hardcover (LB): ISBN: 0-15-200943-4.

Organized by theme, this lavishly illustrated picture book compares stories from diverse religions on topics such as creation, floods, animals, birth, courtship, and marriage. Other sections explore war, pestilence, persecution, and lives of religious leaders. Aimed at elementary-aged students through high school and adult, this text will fascinate you. I found myself wanting to know someone else who was reading it, too, so we could talk about the differences and similarities in world religions. This would be a great choice for a book group to discuss if you are fortunate enough to belong to one. If not, start one and suggest this title. I'd like to have prints of much of the watercolor art from this book—it's so beautiful, that I'd like to frame it and hang it in my office and home. Rich with purples, reds, golds, blues, and greens, the jewel tones tie together the entire collection of stories for a satisfying sense of continuity and truth.

Gilbert, Jane. ***Indescribably Arabella.*** Atheneum, 2003. Hardcover (LB): ISBN 0-689-85321-1.

Arabella knows that she is destined to be famous, but she doesn't know how or doing what. So she tries painting, and acting, and dancing, none of which turns out successfully until she finally learns to be herself. An inspiring story about persistence and individuality.

Goble, Paul. *The Gift of the Sacred Dog.* Bt Bound, 1999.
Hardcover (LB): ISBN 0-808-53585-4.

To the nomadic buffalo hunters of the Great Plains, the horses introduced by the Spanish were truly miraculous animals—strong, swift,
able to carry great burdens long distances. These gifts from the Great
Spirit were called by many names: Big Dog, Elk Dog, Mysterious Dog,
and Sacred Dog. In this richly illustrated book, Paul Goble tells the legend of the Sacred Dog as envisioned through the eyes of the Sioux people. A quiet yet powerful example of voice. (YA)

Hathorn, Libby. *Way Home.* Knopf, 1994. Hardcover: ISBN 0-517-59909-0.

Dark, shadowy pictures torn right from the world of the street combine with passionate but
understated text to create a mood that blends fear, compassion, warmth, hope, and courage.
Follow the boy Shane on a one-night adventure through foreboding alleyways, over fences, past
menacing gangs, and through the blaring noise of street traffic, and feel yourself becoming part
of his world. In brilliant contrast to this stark portrait, author Libby Hathorn fashions a warm
bond between Shane and a small orphaned cat whose name—Catseyes, Bestcat, Catlegs, Hungry,
Noname, Mycat—whimsically changes to reflect his newfound owner's thoughts and moods. In a
striking and unforgettable final image, Hathorn brings new definition to the concept of "home" as
one child of the streets sees and lives it. Passionate and insightful. An original voice.

Hughes, Langston. *The Block.* Viking, 1995. Hardcover: ISBN 0-6708-6501-X.

In his incredible introduction, Bill Cosby summarizes this tribute to Harlem well: "If [Romare]
Bearden shows us the sights, then Langston Hughes gives us the sounds. Street noise and ser-
mons, courting and complaining, rumors and reveries—they are all echoed in these poems of
city life. The voices, too, are familiar. They remind us of our neighbors, our teachers, our
friends." Indeed. This imaginative combination of collage and poetry pulsates with life and the
undeniable rhythm of the street. Come—dance along! Enjoy the rhythm and the voice. Then,
perhaps, ask students to create a collage of their own neighborhood life, a tribute to the sights,
voices, echoes, shadows, and sounds that make up their own world.

I Dream of Peace: Images of War by Children of Former Yugoslavia. UNICEF, HarperCollins,
1994. Hardcover: ISBN 0-06-251128-9.

Captured here in pictures, prose, and poetry are the horrors of war as seen and felt through the
eyes of Yugoslav children. Each section contains vivid imagery of the death and destruction that
is part of everyday life in this war-torn region. This book makes a wonderful companion piece
to *Zlata's Diary,* a 12-year-old's moving day-by-day account of life in the middle of war. (YA)

Johnston, Tony. *Amber on the Mountain.* Bt Bound, 1999. Hardcover (LB): ISBN 0-613-07228-6.

This is a sweet piece that tells the story of a friendship based on reading, books and, most of all,
the value of learning.

Kramer, Stephen P. *Caves.* Carolrhoda Books, 1995. Hardcover (LB): ISBN 0-87614-447-4.
"Far below the earth's surface, water drips from the roof of a cave. The drops fall through darkness into a large stone room no one has ever seen. No bird has ever sung here. The scent of wildflowers has never hung in the air. For thousands of years, the tomblike silence has been broken only by the sound of falling water … Drip … Drip … Drip." Irresistible as the mystery of the cave itself is the newest text by master science writer Steve Kramer. Kramer's friendly text and Kenrick L. Day's outstandingly detailed color photographs bring the world of speleology to rich and vivid life. The author's clear passion for his subject echoes in text that is wonderfully clear and understandable. Use this book to illustrate the value of voice in expository writing, or as an equally fine illustration of technical writing at its best: Kramer makes the complex beautifully penetrable and accessible even to young readers, yet never fails to pique our curiosity. From the history of caves to the diversity found among nature's cave dwellers to the fragile nature of caves themselves, this book has it all. Excellent for ideas and word choice, as well.

Little, Jean. *Hey World, Here I Am!* Bt Bound, 1999. Hardcover (LB): ISBN 0-833-54751-8.
These are essays about life, love, friendship, fear, pride, wins and losses, discovery, parents and children, growing up, and growing old. All the things you think about and care about are probably touched on, in some way, in this marvelous collection of writings that shows us the world through the eyes of young adolescent Kate Bloomfield. Kate is a keen observer of life, and an honest essayist, who dares to tell precisely the truth about any and all topics. Her voice is refreshing, sparkling, daring, and touching. Little captures so well that in-between world of a young person who is beyond childhood but not quite ready to embrace adulthood. The text—some prose, some poetry—will poke you in the ribs one moment and tug at your heart the next. A book to share, to read aloud and to yourself, to treasure, and to give to a friend.

Littlechild, George. *This Land Is My Land.* Children's Book Press, 1993.
Hardcover (LB): ISBN 0-89239-119-7.
"I paint at night. I'm inspired to paint at night. I stand outside staring at the night sky and I begin to dream. The sky is like a doorway into the other world, the Spirit world." In this wonderful collection of Native American art coupled with personal written responses, George Littlechild shows and tells what it means to be a Native American artist about to enter the 21st century. Littlechild's simple, eloquent style reverently depicts Native American customs, traditions, rituals, and history. The book celebrates culture, life, and individual talent. The insights woven throughout the reflective text make this book ideal for introducing introspection and self-reflection, along with the elegant presentation of personal ideas. Littlechild's voice rings with power, yet never overstates the writer's feelings. Like the paintings themselves, the writer's voice retains a quiet dignity that touches the reader's spirit.

Louie, Ai-Ling. *Yeh-Shen: A Cinderella Story From China.* Bt Bound, 1999.
Hardcover (LB): ISBN 0-785-71533-9.

> A collection of famous fairy tales from around the world would have to include this version of Cinderella, which is at least 1,000 years older than the earliest known Western version. Yeh-Shen has a misty, dreamlike air, a much different voice from that heard in other versions you may compare it to. Students will be impressed with the brilliant splendor of the words and illustrations that complement each other beautifully.

MacLachlan, Patricia. *What You Know First.* Joanna Cotler Books (HarperCollins), 1995.
Hardcover: ISBN 0-06-024413-5.

> What do you do when you're a child and your parents decide it's time to move and leave behind all that is so familiar—an ocean of grass, an endless sky, the cottonwood trees? How do you capture all the wonderful memories of the sights and sounds and smells of the things you knew first and love best? This lovingly told story is rich with place and memory. Perfect for an idea of how you find things to write about that really matter to you—the little things that make our lives different from everyone else's.

Matthaei, Gay, and Grutman, Jewel. *The Ledgerbook of Thomas Blue Eagle.* Lickle Publishing, 1996. Hardcover: ISBN 1-56566-063-3.

> "Gorgeous," is often the first word readers utter as they leaf reverently through this remarkable journal of a young Sioux boy's transition into the white world at the Carlisle Indian School. The journal is fiction based on fact; Thomas Blue Eagle is not a real person. Yet, the passion underlying the handwritten words, together with the magnificent and telling pictographs, creates such a feeling of authenticity that the reader is truly transported to another time, place, and experience. Each illustration, each detail, is thoughtfully assembled from actual historical accounts and pictorial records of young Indian children who struggled to move from one world into another while retaining a sense of identity, dignity, and spiritual closeness to the Earth they treasure.

McDonald, Megan. *My House Has Stars.* Orchard Books, 1996. Hardcover: ISBN 0-531-09529-0.

> Collections of thoughts on similar topics but from multiple perspectives are a perfect fit with the trait of voice. However, you might want to consider using a resource like this one for ideas, too. *My House Has Stars* visits homes all over the world: the Philippines, Nepal, Ghana, Japan, the American Southwest, Mongolia, Brazil, and Alaska. Each child's voice echoes the same refrain, "My house has stars," and then describes what that means from their regional and cultural perspective. A sensitive, thoughtful, and genuinely rare book, this piece offers a unified vision of our world through children's eyes and the geography of the earth.

Munsch, Robert N. *The Paper Bag Princess.* Annick Press, 1993.
Hardcover (LB): ISBN 0-920236-82-0.

> Ever wonder how those fairy tale people always stay so clean and neat? In the real world, heroines fall down and get dirty, and that also happens in this tribute-to-realism adventure of the rather inept Prince Ronald and his rescuer, Princess Elizabeth. She's more than a vision in pink. This princess bests dragons, masterminds her own adventures, and knows the difference between a true prince and a shabby imitation. Pokes light fun at some traditions that have been asking for it.

Patterson, Francine. ***Koko's Kitten.*** Bt Bound, 1999. Hardcover (LB): ISBN 0-808-58825-7. Meet Koko, a 13-year-old gorilla who, under the care and loving guidance of scientist Dr. Francine Patterson, becomes strikingly adept at communicating about herself and her world through American Sign Language (ASL). Koko also has a passion for cats, and this fascinating book is dedicated to Koko's pet and companion, All Ball. A remarkable study of animals' ability to use language to express love, anger, need, sorrow, and joy. An excellent example of informational nonfiction writing with voice.

Paulson, Tim. ***Jack and the Beanstalk and the Beanstalk Incident.*** Birch Lane, 1990. Hardcover: ISBN 0-68538-934-0. (Out of print)
The infamous giant takes a stand to clear up a popular misconception about his guilt in the famous fairy tale "Jack and the Beanstalk." In this upside-down fairy tale, you get to read the original as well as the story retold from the giant's point of view. An ingenious way to explore voice with student writers who will quickly see how much voice is dependent on the point of view of the writer. (See also *Cinderella: The Untold Story* by Russell Shorto.)

Polacco, Patricia. ***Aunt Chip and the Great Triple Creek Dam Affair.*** Philomel Books, 1996. Hardcover: ISBN 0-399-22943-4.
"Absolutely everybody in Triple Creek loved their TV sets. No one could remember a time when there wasn't a TV in every home. Nor could they remember when they weren't watching TV." So begins the deliciously wonderful story of *Aunt Chip and the Great Triple Creek Dam Affair.* You see, in this town, books were no longer read; they weren't even used as sources of information. Aunt Chip was the sole holdout. She remembered and even talked about her beloved books and their powerful stories. But for the rest of the town books were doorstops or used to hold the roof up, sit on, or eat off. Can you imagine? This piece is a MUST HAVE in every classroom. The rediscovery of printed words, their power and imagination, is a story that you will want to share with students over and over again. Patricia Polacco is a master at teaching and delighting at the same time. BUY THIS BOOK!

Polacco, Patricia. ***Mrs. Katz and Tush.*** Bantam Books, 1992. Hardcover: ISBN 0-553-08122-5. This heartwarming tale illustrates the suffering and triumph of African American history right alongside Jewish heritage. This story is about respect, appreciation, bonding, and a love that grows from shared experience. The characters are vivid, hopeful, proud, and compassionate.

Polacco, Patricia. ***Pink and Say.*** Philomel Books, 1994. Hardcover (LB): ISBN 0-399-22671-0. The refrain, "This is the hand, that has touched the hand, that has touched the hand, that shook the hand of Abraham Lincoln," will echo through your head and heart long after this historical fiction story ends. A Civil War tale of how a young, frightened, and wounded white solder is saved by a black soldier, this story reminds us of the horrors of war and the inequities of race. Beautifully told, rich with substance and messages of shared humanity. (A three-handkerchief book, and five-star review from our readers; YA)

Ringgold, Faith. *Tar Beach.* Crown, 1991. Hardcover: ISBN 0-517-58030-6.
"I will always remember when the stars fell down around me and lifted me up above the George Washington Bridge." Thus begins the amazing, soaring journey of Cassie Louise Lightfoot, from "Tar Beach," the rooftop of her family's Harlem apartment building, to the George Washington Bridge and beyond, wherever her eight-year-old spirit and imagination will take her. Anyone can fly, Cassie tells us; it's just a matter of longing to be free and claiming the world for your own. Author Faith Ringgold has woven a magical, wondrous tale that is part story, part painting, part traditional quilt. Share the magic of a loving family's tradition that became a poetic tribute to the spirit of a child. (Caldecott Medal winner and the Coretta Scott King Award)

Rosen, Michael J., Ed. *Purr ... Children's Book Illustrators Brag About Their Cats.* Harcourt Brace, 1996. Hardcover (LB): ISBN 0-15-200837-3.
What could be more delightful than the vision of 30 respected and noted children's book illustrators all sharing their perspectives on cats? In this volume, each illustrator shares a favorite picture of a cat and then makes some observations about cats. Some are hilarious, some are thoughtful, and some are insightful. All are different. Students can use this volume to see how many different voices can write about a similar topic. Anthologies are a favorite way to show a variety of voices on a similar topic. (If you are a dog lover, there is a similar volume on dogs, too.)

Rosenberg, Liz. *The Carousel.* Bt Bound, 1999. Hardcover (LB): ISBN 0-613-09939-7.
It's the magic of carousel horses coming to life that leads the two sisters in the story to the realization of the lasting gift of their mother's love. This fantasy story is a charmer. The message is one of courage and adventure, but the entire story with its glorious illustrations, speaks directly to the reader's imagination while capturing the heart.

Ryder, Joanne. *Earthdance.* Bt Bound, 1999. Hardcover (LB): ISBN 0-613-16666-3.
"Imagine you are the Earth. Feel yourself growing taller than the trees, larger than the moon. Imagine you are twirling, dancing through space. You are covered with woods and seas, roads and villages, small creatures and laughing children. Imagine you are home to everyone and everything, the precious place we all know and love best." This poetic book (featured in the *Seeing With New Eyes* video) cries out for dance and movement. Its sensory approach to helping students explore a topic in many different "voices" is environmentally sensitive and a celebration of the planet Earth.

Rylant, Cynthia. *An Angel for Solomon Singer.* Bt Bound, 1999.
Hardcover (LB): ISBN 0-613-09443-3.
One night, Solomon Singer, a mysterious, homeless wanderer and dreamer of things he cannot ever have, finds a small restaurant where—as the menu says—all your dreams come true. "That night, Solomon's face is reflected in a spoon and a waiter's voice, 'quiet like Indiana pines in November,' welcomes him to the Westway Cafe. The waiter's name is Angel." A terrific addition to a set of materials on place, home, or issues relating to the homeless. It is also a good stand-alone piece that invites several plausible interpretations. I think Cynthia Rylant has a great gift for finding important issues and sharing them in a way that allows us to grow and expand our thinking as we ponder them together and apart.

San Souci, Robert D. *Kate Shelley: Bound for Legend.* Dial Books, 1995.
Hardcover (LB): ISBN 0-8037-1290-1.

This true story of Kate Shelley recreates a heroic rescue resulting from a storm and a dreadful train wreck in Iowa in the summer of 1881—from the perspective of the young woman herself. I love this piece because we have so few historical pieces written from a woman's perspective, especially pieces that young as well as older children can read and enjoy.

Scieszka, Jon. *The Frog Prince, Continued.* Viking Press, 1991.
Hardcover (LB): ISBN 0-670-83421-1.

You may think you know the story of the Frog Prince, but you'll have to read on to find out the shocking truth about life "happily ever after." In much the same voice as *The Paper Bag Princess,* this tale takes unpredictable twists and turns on its way to the true meaning of love and happiness. This is a long way from the Brothers Grimm!

Scieszka, Jon. *Math Curse.* Viking Press, 1995. Hardcover (LB): ISBN 0-670-86194-4.

The minute this book hit the shelves it was prized by teachers and kids alike. At every workshop people say, "Oh, I have that. Isn't it the greatest?" If, by some remote chance, you haven't seen this clever and typically original Scieszka book, run to your nearest library. If you've ever suffered from math anxiety, you'll relate immediately. If you've ever struggled to help kids understand how they use the things they learn in everyday life, you'll love it. If you just want to be amazed by someone's original ideas and incredible imagination, read it with pleasure and delight.

Scieszka, Jon. *The Stinky Cheese Man and Other Fairly Stupid Tales.* Viking, 1993.
Hardcover (LB): ISBN 0-670-84487-X.

Get ready for a ride. Scieszka wags his irreverent tongue from cover to cover in this delightful romp through some once-familiar fairy tales. From the "Really Ugly Duckling" to "Jack's Bean Problem," students will be thoroughly entertained. Older students will appreciate the sarcasm and black humor. Students of all ages will find themselves inspired to put their personal stamp on familiar tales. (YA)

Seattle, Chief. *Brother Eagle, Sister Sky: A Message From Chief Seattle.* Dial Books, 1991.
Library Binding: ISBN 0-8037-0963-3.

"How can you buy the sky?" "How can you own the rain and the wind?" So began the moving words attributed to a great American Indian Chief more than 100 years ago. They are the words that eloquently and poetically captured the central belief of Native Americans: That this earth and every creature on it are sacred. Susan Jeffers's extraordinary paintings masterfully illuminate the words and world vision of Native Americans. (YA)

Sendak, Maurice. *We Are All in the Dumps With Jack and Guy.* HarperCollins, 1993.
Hardcover: ISBN 0-06-205014-1.

Based on two nursery rhymes, this provocative picture book confronts the issue of homeless children. The illustrations draw you into the text while carefully weaving powerful messages about despair, poverty, richness, and excess into the reader's mind. An excellent example of voice with conviction achieved through very few words.

Shimmel, Schim. *Dear Children of the Earth.* NorthWord Press, 1994.
Hardcover: ISBN 1-55971-225-2.

> The first thing to catch your eye will be the surrealistic paintings of the earth, its creatures and its beauty. The second will be the poignant words that cry out for our children to learn about the beauty of the Earth, how fragile she is, and how they will, one day very soon, become her caretakers. Written in letter format from the Earth to the children, this piece is a powerful example of a topic that students have passion about and a great place for a writing assignment as they create thoughtful, information-packed responses.

Stewart, Sarah. *The Journey.* Farrar, Straus and Giroux, 2001. Hardcover: ISBN 0-374-33905-8.

> This is a gentle story of discovery and contrast as young Amish girl Hannah makes a journey to Chicago, leaving her small and simple community for the first time. Hannah writes to us (her silent friends) through her diary, providing glimpses of wonder and recalled memories as she experiences the fascinating sights of the big city. Students will enjoy talking about Hannah's "voice," so strong in one so young.

Thaler, Mike. *The Teacher From the Black Lagoon.* Bt Bound, 1999.
Hardcover (LB): ISBN 0-8335-4273-7.

> Who will get a bigger charge out of this book—kids or teachers? Mike Thaler knows well what lurks deep in the hearts of kids and teachers as he capitalizes on the nervous excitement and fear that come with meeting your teacher on the first day of school. Characters of the absurd strike a chord with adults and children alike as Mrs. Green wreaks chaos and mayhem with her young students in the classroom. Gross and wildly exaggerated, this book is an all-time favorite. This is one time we don't seem to mind the "and I woke up and it was only a dream" ending. Ask students what kind of voice this writer is using and why it is so effective. Ask them under what circumstances they would use this kind of voice, and what the hallmarks are of doing it well. (*Principal From the Black Lagoon* and *School Bus Driver From the Black Lagoon* also available.)

Vieira, Linda. *The Ever-Living Tree: Life and Times of a Coast Redwood.* Walker, 1994.
Hardcover (LB): ISBN 0-8027-8278-7.

> A workshop participant recommended this piece to me. He said he used it with his students to show how detailed information can be written in an interesting way that moves the reader through the text. There's a tremendous amount of information about the life cycle of the redwood tree in this text, but it is brought to life through thoughtfully written sections and always, always with the reader in mind. I'd use this book as a contrast to the bleak vagueness of the original and now infamous "Redwoods" piece from the six-trait workshop. This comparison could motivate students to investigate topics of their own and then write about them with the energy and authenticity modeled in this picture book.

Vos Wezeman, Phyllis. *Benjamin Brody's Backyard Bag.* Brethren Press, 1991.
Hardcover: ISBN 0-87178-091-7.

> Another in the collection of stories dealing with the homeless, this story is different in its approach from *Fly Away Home* by Eve Bunting, *We Are All in the Dumps With Jack and Guy* by Maurice Sendak, or *Seeing Eye Willie* by Dale Gottlieb. This story carefully develops the theme of "home" as it explores the thoughtful, practical, and very realistic point of view of young Benjamin Brody.

Yolen, Jane. *Sleeping Ugly.* Bt Bound, 1999. Hardcover (LB): ISBN 0-8085-8544-4.
When selfish Princess Miserella—beautiful on the surface only—meets the charming and modest Plain Jane—beautiful inside, where it counts—major changes rattle the timbers of the proverbial little house in the woods (where the floors are sinking and the walls are stinking). In this nontraditional fairy tale, you'll also encounter a prince who requires a bit of coaching before he can make the right princely choices, and an old fairy godmother with enough chutz-pah to give the Miserellas of the world the comeuppance they so richly deserve.

Passion is to picture books as yeast is to bread: one is nothing without the other ....
Writing without passion is writing for oblivion.
—Mem Fox, *Dear Mem Fox, I Have Read All Your Books Even the Pathetic Ones*

Word Choice

Deliciously used everyday words
Wordsmithery and word pictures
Precision and growth with language

Adoff, Arnold. ***Sports Pages.*** HarperCollins, 1986. Hardcover (LB): ISBN 0-39-732102-3.
  Do you have students who love sports but can't see poetry for dust? Turn them on to a new way of thinking with this wonderful book in which those two worlds meet. Rhythmic and musical, yet enlivened with the authentic language of the sports world, this gem of a book superbly captures the poetry of playing hard and well. Pssst … wonderful for sentence fluency, too. (NCTE Award for Excellence in Poetry for Children)

Alexander, Lloyd. ***How the Cat Swallowed Thunder.*** Dutton Books, 2000.
Paperback: ISBN 0-525-46449-2.
  The author is well-known for his fantasy stories, and this book is no exception. Mother Holly leaves her cottage in the capable hands of Cat, but Cat is a rascal and decides that taking a nap is much more attractive than doing housework. Cat's nap is endlessly postponed, however, by a rain shower, thunder, windstorm, and snow—all inside the cottage! How could this be? A book to keep older listeners guessing. (YA)

Alvarez, Julia. ***The Secret Footprints.*** Knopf, 2000. Hardcover (LB): ISBN 0-679-99309-6.
  This story is based on a Dominican folk tale about the secretive Ciguapas people who live in the sea and have their feet on backward. Guapa is an adventurous young lady, whose curiosity nearly leads to discovery and disaster. Colorful illustrations add to this legend's mystery.

Ashman, Linda. ***Rub-a-Dub Sub.*** Harcourt, 2003. Hardcover (LB): ISBN 0-15-202658-4.
  In the rhyming tradition of Dr. Seuss, Linda Ashman takes us on a colorful journey under the sea to encounter all kinds of creatures with strange shapes and names. Youngsters will enjoy both the rhyme and the adventure in this imaginative tale.

Baker, Keith. ***The Magic Fan.*** Bt Bound, 1999. Hardcover (LB): ISBN 0-613-02348-X.
  Written to inspire imagination in all ages, this Japanese folk tale tells the story of Yoshi who builds a boat to catch the moon, a kite to catch the clouds, and a bridge to save the village from a powerful tsunami. The language is poetic and yet clearly conveys the tone and voice of the piece. Powerful verbs, precise nouns … Baker is a writer who knows how to use language well. See also (for younger readers) *Who Is the Beast?* by the same author. A special thank-you to sharp-eyed Gaye Lantz of Tacoma, Washington, for spotting this author's fine works and sharing them with us.

Base, Graeme. *My Grandma Lived in Gooligulch.* Abrams, 1990. Hardcover: ISBN 0-8109-1547-2. Here's a terrific tale in rollicking verse and marvelously detailed illustrations from one of the best, Australian author Graeme Base. Invite students to enjoy this story by pulling out unfamiliar words *(billabong, galahs, kookaburras, wombat,* etc.) from the text to see if they can figure out what these intriguing words mean. Reread this story aloud several times and ask if the words and images have changed in any way since the first reading.

Brown, Marc. *Arthur's Teacher Moves In.* Little, Brown, 2000. Hardcover: ISBN 0-316-11979-2. The new guest at Arthur's house causes alarm when it turns out to be his teacher. Having Mr. Ratburn in his house is not as difficult, though, as dealing with the new attitude of his friends who think Arthur has turned into the "teacher's pet." When he hears of the problem, Mr. Ratburn takes care of it in a clever way. A good lesson in the dangers of making assumptions about people.

Burdett, Lois. *A Midsummer Night's Dream for Kids.* Firefly Books, 1997. Hardcover: ISBN 1-55209-130-9.

From world-class teacher and author Lois Burdett, *A Midsummer Night's Dream* just keeps on amazing and astounding. (Find her other books listed under the trait of ideas.) The quality of the writing and the "wordsmithery" done by her seven- and eight-year-olds is truly remarkable. Listen to this example: *"Puck had made a dredful BOO-BOO! He put the love juice into Lysander's eyes. Heleaa came blubering by with a pudel of tear behind her. Lysander saw Helena and fell in love. Hermia is left with a crack up heart! That makes confewshun!"* This piece, along with her others, makes wonderful examples to show students at all ages how the traits of word choice and voice work so well together.

Clements, Andrew. *Double Trouble in Walla Walla.* Millbrook Press, 1997. Hardcover (LB): ISBN 0-7613-0306-5.

Everything was tip-top in Walla Walla until it became a big mish-mash. When LuLu raised her hand in class and her teacher called on her, an onslaught of flip-flop chit-chat began. And it was contagious! So much so they had to trit-trot down to the principal's office to see what all the hub-bub was about. Mrs. Bell, the teacher, explained, "LuLu's been trying to razzle-dazzle me with some kind of lippity-loppity jibber-jabber, and now I'm all helter-skelter myself." And so the story unfolds until the teacher, principals, and Lulu come up with a VERY unusual cure. Eeeka-freaka! It's really DOUBLE TROUBLE IN WALLA WALLA!

dePaola, Tomie. *Adelita: A Mexican Cinderella Story.* Putnam's Sons, 2002. Hardcover (LB): ISBN 0-399-23866-2.

The classic fairy tale is retold in Mexico with a rebozo, or shawl, playing the part of the glass slipper that finally brings the couple together. Tomie dePaola has cleverly woven Spanish into the text, and the illustrations provide a true Mexican folk art atmosphere. (YA)

Duffield, Katy S. ***Farmer McPeepers and His Missing Milk Cows.*** Rising Moon, 2003. Hardcover (LB): 0-87358-825-8.

Farmer McPeepers embarks on a search for his missing milk cows, but unfortunately does not take time to pick up his glasses. He passes fishermen, swimmers, and even movie-goers but never catches sight of his cows. Until he gets home that is, and puts on his glasses. The humor of the story is enhanced by the hilarious, cartoon-style illustrations of Steve Gray.

Ering, Timothy Basil. ***The Story of Frog Belly Rat Bone.*** Candlewick Press, 2003. Hardcover (LB): ISBN 0-7636-1382-7.

A strange metal box reveals a treasure that turns the dreariness of Cementland into a colorful kingdom. Evocative acrylic illustrations add to the atmosphere of this unusual tale.

Fox, Mem. ***Feathers and Fools.*** Harcourt Brace, 1996. Hardcover (LB): ISBN 0-15-200473-4.

I haven't found a book that has grabbed hold of my heart and mind as much as this masterpiece by Mem Fox. The language is sophisticated and eloquent. Passages such as "Again the first peacock spoke. 'How strange that swans should fly. It is happy indeed that we do not, for we should surely look ridiculous.' The other peacocks pecked and strutted again, contemplating the meaning of this second observation."

This piece was written in 1989 but illustrated in 1996. It was worth the wait, Mem. As always, you are true to your belief that children need words and images in their minds before they can express themselves clearly. Once again you honor them with a piece that will fill their heads with pictures, words, and ideas. The message couldn't be more timely or brought home more clearly with the perfect marriage of text and pictures. A third, fourth, and fifth reading only serve to underscore its truth. Like the peacocks and swans in this story, we humans are quick to use our differences as a source of distrust that has led not only to wars, but also to the ongoing struggle for peace in neighborhoods, cities, and regions around the world. This book would be well-paired with *Smoky Nights* and/or *Pink and Say.* (YA)

Fox, Mem. ***Possum Magic.*** Bt Bound, 1999. Hardcover (LB): ISBN 0-833-58190-2.

Here's another Mem Fox favorite. At times using rhyme and gentle alliteration to create pictures in our minds, this simple story charms us with words and phrases we love and remember. "It was there, in the far north of Australia, that they found a Vegemite sandwich. Grandma Poss crossed her claws and crossed her feet. Hush breathed deeply and began to eat. 'A tail! A tail!' shouted both possums at once. For there it was. A brand new, visible tail." A good choice for sentence fluency, too, with engaging rhythm achieved through sentence variety and well-placed fragments.

Gambling, Louise G. ***The Witch Who Wanted To Be a Princess.*** Whispering Coyote Press, 2002. Hardcover (LB): ISBN 1-58089-062-8.

Bella is a modern witch in every way, except that she has the age-old dream of becoming a princess. Even graduating top of her witches' training class doesn't give her the power to transform herself, so she does the next best thing—she sets out to marry a handsome prince. Clever illustrations add to the humor of this tale with a twist at the end.

Garland, Sherry. ***The Lotus Seed.*** Harcourt Brace, 1993. Hardcover (LB): ISBN 0-15-249465-0. Do you believe that simple words are often best? If so, you will not want to miss this power-house tale of love, fear, loss, and hope. A young Vietnamese girl emigrates from a homeland torn apart by war, with only a lotus seed to remind her of the traditions and memories left so far behind. Years later, a young child, not knowing the significance of the lotus flower, takes the seed, then loses it. See how much this family discovers as they search for a tiny seed that symbolizes more to them than anyone had realized. This is a story beautifully told. Its simple yet well-conceived plot makes it an excellent example of organization as well.

Gerstein, Mordicai. ***The Absolutely Awful Alphabet.*** Harcourt Brace, 1999. Hardcover (LB): ISBN 0-15-201494-2.
Start with an awfully arrogant amphibian and end with a zigzagging zoological zany; put in all the crazy letters between and there you have this absolutely awful alphabet that stretches the limits of word wizardry. A great example of using words to create vivid images.

Harshman, Marc. ***The Storm.*** Cobblehill Books (Dutton), 1995. Hardcover: ISBN 0-525-65150-0. Listen to this section from an amazing work which could be used in EVERY trait: "Jonathan looked again at the sky. And there he saw it, saw the strange, black thumb press itself down out of the bulging mass of clouds and stretch into a narrow tongue just licking over the surface of the ground. Tornado!" *The Storm* is all about tornadoes, but even more, it is about a young man's struggle to be seen as himself, not as "the boy in the wheelchair." The adventure of *The Storm* provides Jonathan an opportunity to do more than he ever realized he could, and to help others see him as the person he is becoming. Nicely written and speaks to us all. I think you'll like this one!

Heller, Ruth. ***Many Luscious Lollipops.*** Bt Bound, 1999. Hardcover (LB): ISBN 0-833-59165-7. Buy it for the illustrations alone, and enjoy this painless tour through the world of adjectives. This is one of a series by Heller, which includes books specializing in verbs, nouns, and adverbs. Captivating and creative, with a style all its own.

Hundal, Nancy. ***Twilight Fairies.*** Fitzhenry & Whiteside, 2002. Hardcover: ISBN 1-55041-645-6. Miranda's mid-summer birthday will be different this year. She has chosen to have a garden party at twilight instead of the usual bowling or sleepover. And along with her school friends she has also invited the fairy folk who live in her garden. Will they all come? Whether you believe in the little people or not, this story will reawaken simple dreams of childhood.

Jennings, Sharon. ***Priscilla's Paw de Deux.*** Fitzhenry & Whiteside, 2002. Hardcover: ISBN 1-55041-718-5.
Priscilla Mouse's ballet dreams are severely hampered by the smallness of her mouse hole. So she goes hole-hunting, only to come across a real ballet school complete with watch-cat. An obstacle turns into an asset, however, and Priscilla finds herself a most unusual (for a mouse) dancing partner.

Joosse, Barbara M. *I Love You the Purplest.* Chronicle Books, 1996.
Hardcover: ISBN: 0-8118-0718-5.

> A wise mother indeed knows the not-so-subtle traps her children lay for her in an attempt to reinforce how much they are loved. The two boys in this story are no exception. "Who do you love most, Mom?" is the refrain echoed over and over in this book in different contexts. During a summer fishing trip, the mother artfully finds the right words to point out the wonderful qualities each child possesses—never putting one above the other, but always finding a way to make each feel special. "Julian, I love you the bluest. I love you the color of a dragon fly at the tip of the wind … and Max, I love you the reddest. I love you the color of the sky before it blazes into night …." A tender, delightful, and heartwarming book. If I could only take two books with me to a workshop (yeah, right—like THAT is ever going to happen) this would be one of them. The other? *Hoops* by Robert Burleigh. Well then, of course I couldn't live without my Mem Fox books, either ….

Kay, Verla. *Gold Fever.* G.P. Putnam, 1999. Hardcover (LB): ISBN 0-399-23027-0.

> Jasper the farmer decides to head to California when he hears of the gold that can be found there. But all is not as easy as it sounds, and he finds that the life of a digger has many drawbacks, such as snakes and grizzlies, grumpy miners, and costly provisions. A cautionary tale, written in poetic form, about the grass being greener over the hill. Also good for the trait of sentence fluency.

Krull, Kathleen. *Wilma Unlimited: How Wilma Rudolph Became the World's Fastest Woman.*
Raintree/Steck Vaughn, 2000. Hardcover (LB): ISBN 0-7398-1321-8.

> Born and raised in Clarksville, Tennessee, Wilma loved to run and play until she became very ill with polio, which left her unable to walk. She never gave up trying, however, and even after doctors said it was impossible, she walked on her own and eventually won three gold Olympic medals. This is a book of inspiration and sheer human tenacity. Coupled with David Diaz's *(Smoky Nights)* illustrations, I felt the anguish and struggle of Wilma's life and celebrated right along with her as she triumphed. The author's style adds drama and flair to this biography and helps you to personalize Wilma's experiences.

Kurtz, Jane. *Faraway Home.* Gulliver Books, 2000. Hardcover: ISBN 0-15-200036-4.

> This poignant story is about living in one world while being emotionally connected to another. Desta's dad is drawn back to his homeland of Ethiopia, a land that she knows little about and is fearful of. Will he return safely? A great example of fear of the strange and unknown that will have your students revealing their own thoughts and fears. Use it to explore how background and experience influence how we act. (YA)

Leaf, Munro. *The Story of Ferdinand.* Viking, 1964. Hardcover (LB): ISBN 0-670-67424-9.

> Spanish bullfights rely on a powerful, energetic bull. So when Ferdinand is chosen to fight in the famous bullring in Madrid, he is expected to put on a good show. But Ferdinand prefers to sit in the shade and smell the flowers on the hats of the ladies, which is not what the Matador needs at all. This traditional story has been a favorite for more than 50 years. The language choice and black and white line illustrations help create a classic book.

Lewis, Paul Owen. **Storm Boy.** Gareth Stevens, 1999. Hardcover (LB): ISBN 0-836822-29-3.
Wow! The artwork alone from the rugged Northwest coast and its native Haida, Tlingit, and other Native American tribal people make this a stand-alone work. Beyond that, however, is a story with precise historical detail and a sense of mystery. It reads like poetry, and deepens one's understanding and appreciation for the beauty of the Native American traditions.

Locker, Thomas. **Mountain Dance.** Silver Whistle, 2001. Hardcover (LB): ISBN 0-15-202622-3.
This book captures the magic and grandeur of the ever-changing land around us. Using lyrical but scientifically accurate vocabulary accompanied by beautiful illustrations, the author provides us with a glimpse of the role and power of wind, rain, and sun in the formation of mountains. Also good for the trait of ideas.

Lounsbury, Charles. **Pictures in the Fire.** Laughing Elephant, 2003.
Hardcover: ISBN 0-9621-1319-0.
I believe this book is true. I know, I know, it could all be created by the publisher, but deep in my heart, I want to believe someone was good enough to know that the true riches of the world lie less in how much we have when we die than the way we leave the world at the end of our time here. Mr. Lounsbury's last will and testament "found" by the publisher and legally probated by the Chicago Bar Association leaves the world all the good things by reminding us of what they are. His special emphasis on the beauty and love of children is poignant and moving. The words, though a bit archaic for our time, speak clearly and eloquently. I dare you to read this and not want to believe it is true! (YA)

Lum, Kate. **Princesses Are Not Quitters.** Bloomsbury, 2002. Hardcover: ISBN 1-58234-762-X.
Having taken on the tasks of their servants for a day, three princesses fight off exhaustion and come to understand that some workers don't have it so good. Will the experience cause them to make changes? A cleverly constructed story of determination enhanced by the line illustrations of Sue Hellard.

Lund, Deb. **Dinosailors.** Harcourt, 2003. Hardcover (LB): ISBN 0-15-204609-7.
Dinosailors take to the sea, but maybe that is not where they belong. Their cruise turns into a nightmare as they learn the realities of storms and a constantly rocking boat that could turn anyone green. Perhaps they belong on land after all …? A beautifully illustrated story.

Martin, Bill Jr. **A Beasty Story.** Silver Whistle, 1999. Hardcover: ISBN 0-15-201683-X.
Bill Martin and illustrator Steven Kellogg collaborate to produce wonderfully rhythmic text and visually engaging pictures in this story of creepy settings and growing tension, as four diminutive heroes explore the "dark, dark house." Use it with younger writers to discover the power of descriptive words.

Maruki, Toshi. *Hiroshima No Pika.* William Morrow, 1982.
Hardcover: ISBN 0-688-01297-3.

> This simple, yet elegant and moving text describes the events of Hiroshima on August 6, 1945. The specific use of language and carefully designed flow of the text underscore the monumental series of events as they unfolded that fateful day at Hiroshima. The illustrations build in intensity from page to page until the enormity of the event becomes part of your very soul. An important book that received numerous honors including the prestigious Boston Globe/Horn Book Award. (YA)

Marzollo, Jean. *I Spy Extreme Challenger.* Cartwheel Books, 2000.
Hardcover: ISBN 0-439-19900-X.

> Latest in the *I Spy* series, *Extreme Challenger* provides all the fun and challenge that the name implies. The authors bury their objects in a host of wonderful pictures that stand alone as fabulous collections of fascinating trinkets. I spent hours just mesmerized by the pictures! Useful for developing vocabulary and for getting ideas started.

Monceaux, Morgan. *Jazz: My Music, My People.* Knopf, 1994.
Hardcover: ISBN 0-679-85618-8.

> This is an inspired combination of bold, eye-catching paintings, reflective memories, and biographies of some of the world's great jazz artists and history makers. Artists like W.C. Handy, Bessie Smith, Ethel Waters, Louis Armstrong, Dizzie Gillespie, Nat King Cole, Sarah Vaughn, Lena Horne, Pearl Bailey, and many others come to life on pages that celebrate their extraordinary talent. This marvelous behind-the-scenes look at the world of jazz opens with a foreword by Wynton Marsalis highlighting *The Legend of Buddy Bolden:* "So confidently did Bolden's sound shout out against the gumbo-thick New Orleans sky that people way across the Mississippi River in Algiers could clearly hear that it was time to swing with a happiness that infected all within earshot." You'll swing with happiness, too, as you encounter masterfully crafted phrasing and wonderfully choice detail on every page. (YA)

Musgrove, Margaret. *Ashanti to Zulu: African Traditions.* Bt Bound, 1999.
Hardcover (LB): ISBN 0-8810-3864-4.

> Here's a beautifully illustrated alphabet book, one you'll savor for its original text and even more for the exceptional pictures. A glorious celebration of African traditions. "The Dillons's paintings are breathtaking recreations of tribal life, authentic in detail and spirit as well. The tribes are arranged alphabetically, making this an advanced ABC book as well .... Carefully researched and skillfully executed."—*Chicago Sun Times* (Caldecott Medal winner)

Myers, Walter Dean. *Blues Journey.* Holiday House, 2003. Hardcover: ISBN 0-8234-1613-5.

> An unusual combination of emotive illustrations and blues lyrics, this book reflects America's musical art form through the black experience of sharecropping, prison work-gangs, and lynchings. It is a powerful story that will be enjoyed by older readers for both its message and its form. (YA)

Oppenheim, Joanne. *Have You Seen Trees?* Scholastic, 1995.
Hardcover (LB): ISBN 0-590-46691-7.
> This descriptive piece is about the moods, feelings, sights, and sounds of trees and their leaves through all the seasons. "Dry leaves, brown leaves, covering-the-ground leaves. Make-a-crunching-sound leaves, dropping-everywhere leaves, left-the-trees-bare leaves. I can hear the crunch of the crisp dry leaves!" This would also be a good book to share about the creative use of conventions. This book is a great descriptive writing prompt. See what your kids can do with the sights and sounds of the seasons after they hear this author's ideas.

Palatini, Margie. *Earthquack.* Simon & Schuster, 2002. Hardcover (LB): ISBN 0-689-84280-5.
> Using the theme of Henny Penny's falling sky, the author has created a clever story of imagined quaking earth, a panicky rumor started by little Chucky Ducky. This book combines humorous illustrations with clever word play to create a rollicking tale. Also good for organization.

Park, Barbara. *Psssst! It's Me … the Bogeyman.* Atheneum Books, 1998.
Hardcover (LB): ISBN 0-689-81667-7.

> Don't read this book on a dark night on your own! Seriously, this is a bogeyman who wants to clear his name and set the record straight about who does all the scaring around town. And it isn't him … or so he says. Clever, up-to-the-minute language will keep young readers enthralled and smiling through this tongue-in-cheek account of a bogeyman's bad day, or should that be night?

Pinkey, Sandra L. *Shades of Black: A Celebration of Our Children.* Scholastic, 2000.
Hardcover (LB): ISBN 0-439-14892-8.
> From black to creamy white, this book celebrates the diversity of African American children. Using the poetry of metaphor, Sandra Pinkey moves from skin color to hair texture to flashing, mischievous eyes to describe the pride that there is in our heritage. A wonderful introduction to diversity and tolerance for younger listeners. Also good for the trait of sentence fluency.

Plourde, Lynn. *Wild Child.* Aladdin Paperbacks, 1999. Hardcover (LB): ISBN 0-689-81552-2.
> A story of the seasons is wrapped up in the familiar images of a youngster heading, eventually, to bed. The poetic form and the autumnal sounds of the words will capture the imaginations of young listeners. Also good for the trait of sentence fluency.

Raschka, Chris. *Yo! Yes?* Orchard Books, 1993. Hardcover: ISBN 0-531-05469-1.
> Two boys meet on the street and through the simplest of dialogue, "Yo!" "Yes?" explore the tentative beginnings of a friendship. In this Caldecott Honor picture book, everyday words convey a multitude of meanings through inflection, placement, and presentation. Students may wish to explore other pairings of words in stories of their own.

Robbins, Ken. *Earth: The Elements.* Henry Holt, 1995. Hardcover: ISBN 0-8050-2294-5.
This simple and beautiful book of geological elements makes you want to drop everything and run to the nearest igneous rock just to check it out. Visually stunning photographs coupled with eloquent expository prose. Similar to its sister book, *Water:* "An elegant change from the more 'efficiently' written and illustrated science books …. The pictures are a cool drink in an often arid genre." —*The Bulletin of the Center for Children's Books.* (YA)

Rylant, Cynthia. *Appalachia: The Voices of Sleeping Birds.* Bt Bound, 1999.
Hardcover (LB): ISBN 0-613-10494-3.
This exquisite volume illustrates the moods, sounds, and feel of the Appalachian region. It invites you to explore the beauty of the countryside, the simple majesty of the people. The prose and illustrations help you to imagine life and traditions in Appalachia; the words are straight from the heart and chosen to bring this special place to life. If you are collecting books on the theme of place, don't forget this one. The recipient of many, many awards and celebrations including the Parent's Choice Award.

Rylant, Cynthia. *The Dreamer.* Blue Sky Press (Scholastic), 1993.
Hardcover (LB): ISBN 0-590-47341-7. (Out of print)
Perhaps the book jacket says it best, "This is the story of one who dreamed the world." It's a creation story that wraps us all in its warm and simple elegance. Phrases like "Green grass. He painted soft, sweet-smelling green grass—as young artists will almost always do—he got carried away and painted some trees." Coupled with Barry Moser's award-winning watercolors, this book is a treasure.

Rylant, Cynthia. *The Old Woman Who Named Things.* Harcourt Brace, 1996.
Hardcover (LB): ISBN 0-15-257809-9.
How important is just the right name, anyway? Ask the old lady in this delightful story who has outlived all her friends and now only names things in life she knows she can never outlive: her house Franklin, her bed Roxanne, and Bud, the ceramic pig out in her garden. But what to do about the stray dog that faithfully shows up at her garden gate every day? If she doesn't name it, then she doesn't have to worry about outliving it, right? But, as you can imagine, that resolve doesn't last long and the conclusion is a warm and thoughtful treatment of a charming old lady's decision to keep and name the stray who has come into her life. Students would have a lot of fun writing their own stories and naming the important inanimate objects in their lives, too. The stories behind the names will tell a lot!

Scieszka, Jon. *Baloney (Henry P.).* Viking, 2001. Hardcover: ISBN 0-670-89248-3.
If you have ever had to quickly come up with a reason for being late, then you will relate to Henry P. Baloney. He is in trouble with his teacher, and his excuse is out of this world. While you are following this tale of woe, you will also be introduced to his unusual language. See if you can decipher his words (without peeking at the decoder). A great resource for investigating the use of words.

Soto, Gary. ***The Old Man and His Door.*** Bt Bound, 1999. Hardcover (LB): ISBN 0-613-10447-1. Another gift from one of the most prominent voices in Latino-American literature for young people, this delightful story uses English and Spanish to tell its tale. An old man who is very good at working in his garden but terrible at listening to his wife is asked to go get *el puerco,* (the pig). But instead, the old man gets very distracted and brings back *la puerta* (the door). The adventure is charming and funny and all turns out well—even better than anyone could have expected. Sprinkled with Spanish words throughout, a Spanish-to-English glossary is provided right at the front of the story. Wouldn't this be a great idea for students in your class to try and imitate? Help them think up pairs of words that sound very much alike but mean something quite different. Then encourage them to create stories that show how important it is to listen well so the meaning of the words doesn't cause confusion as it did in *The Old Man and His Door.* The stories could be like this one, which uses Spanish and English, or they could use other languages as well.

Stanley, Diane. ***Raising Sweetness.*** Putnam, 1999. Hardcover (LB): ISBN 0-399-23225-7. Here's another story in the saga of the sheriff of Possum Trot and his adopted family. This time the kids are determined to get him married, if only to save themselves from the attentions of Mrs. Sump, who has taken over as their substitute teacher at school. But the only way to accomplish their mission is to learn to read, and therein lies a tale. Enjoy the Texas accent, too!

Steig, William. ***Amos and Boris.*** Bt Bound, 1999. Hardcover (LB): ISBN 0-808-52709-6. They're not the likeliest of friends: Amos, a tiny mouse with an adventuring spirit as large as the world that beckons him, and Boris, a gigantic but gentle whale with an abundant curiosity about life on land. They meet through a series of misadventures—not just once, but twice in their lives; and through their chance meetings forge a bond of friendship no time or circumstance can undo. This is an inspiring story of courage, friendship, and trust, rich with the lyrical language of which Steig is the undeniable master: "Boris admired the delicacy, the quivering daintiness, the light touch, the small voice, the gemlike radiance of the mouse. Amos admired the bulk, the grandeur, the power, the purpose, the rich voice, and the abounding friendliness of the whale." Wonderful as it is for word choice, you'll want to use this delightful picture book for ideas, organization, sentence fluency, and voice, as well.

Steig, William. ***Brave Irene.*** Bt Bound, 1999. Hardcover (LB): ISBN 0-8335-0291-3. "She pounced and took hold, but the ill-tempered wind ripped the box open. The ball gown flounced out and went waltzing through the powdered air with tissue paper attendants." So goes the adventure of the determined, not-to-be-thwarted Irene, who braves wind, cold, and snow to deliver her mother's painstakingly sewn masterpiece gown to the duchess in time for the castle holiday ball. Glorious verbs, vibrant images—all the wonders of word choice we've come to expect from the word wizard himself.

Steig, William. ***Caleb and Kate.*** Farrar, Straus and Giroux, 1977.
Hardcover: ISBN 0-3743-1016-5.

How do you explain to your wife, with whom you've just quarreled, that while you were stomping about in the woods trying to regain your composure, a mischievous witch transformed you into a loving, companionable dog? "Caleb went crashing into the forest by their house, pondering why he had married such a cantankerous hoddy-doddy; but after he'd walked a while, his fury faded and he couldn't remember what it was they had quarreled about." Cantankerous hoddy-doddy? You have to love such out-of-the-ordinary language—colorful, bright, witty, and vivid. This book is as satisfying as a cup of hot cocoa by the fire on a rainy day.

Steig, William. ***Shrek!*** Bt Bound, 1999. Hardcover (LB): ISBN 0-7857-2221-1.

"A mischievous, topsy-turvy chronicle of nasty ogre's wonder years"—*Parenting.*

This book, like all of William Steig's work, exemplifies the degree of sophistication an author can achieve by precise word choice. Never talking down to students, William Steig delights and amazes the reader with his visual pictures, his clever phrasing, and vivid descriptions. Read this one aloud—it's a hoot!

Steig, William. ***Solomon: The Rusty Nail.*** Bt Bound, 1999.
Hardcover (LB): ISBN 0-8335-9906-2.

Solomon is smarter than the average rabbit; in fact, this crafty little character can transform himself into a rusty nail whenever he wants.
Great fun till he's discovered by the unscrupulous cat Ambrose and his wife Clorinda. A deadly dilemma ensues: Should Solomon remain safely in his rusty nail state—indefinitely? Or return to life as a rabbit and risk being turned into rabbit stew? Have some fun working through this sticky problem with the ingeniously resourceful Solomon. A book with personality—like all of Steig's work.

Thompson, Kay, and Crowley, Mart. ***Eloise Takes a Bawth.*** Simon & Schuster, 2002.
Hardcover (LB): ISBN 0-689-84288-0.

Forty years in the drawing (her bath that is), Eloise's "bawth" turns into a disaster for the Plaza Hotel and the Venetian Masked Ball in the "Grawnd" Ballroom. Or does it? A little bit of imagination and ingenuity might just turn the tables and make a tragedy into a triumph, and get Eloise off the hook. This book, the latest (and possibly the last) in the *Eloise* series, was produced from the late Kay Thompson's 1960s manuscript.

Walker, Alice. *To Hell With Dying.* Voyager (Harcourt Brace), 1988.
Hardcover (LB): ISBN 0-15-289075-0.

All of us should have a Mr. Sweet in our lives. In this compelling piece, the main character interacts with an elderly man who often has very bad spells and fears for his life. The family encourages him to hang on, as the father says, "To hell with dying. These children need Mr. Sweet." And slowly, their love and need for him bring Mr. Sweet back to health. Although this continues to be the cycle of life for Mr. Sweet and his friends, many years later, as the main character leaves home for school, there comes the inevitable day when Mr. Sweet does not rise from his sickbed. "He was like a piece of rare and delicate china which was always being saved from breaking and which finally fell." This piece deals with the significance of life and death and the legacy of those who are most significant in our lives. Magnificently written. Well, what else would you expect from Alice Walker?

Yaccarino, Dan. *Deep in the Jungle.* Atheneum Books, 2000. Hardcover: ISBN 0-689-82235-9.
Never trust a person who says "Trust me" is the message of this clever story of a lion who runs afoul of a slick-tongued circus trainer. But a slick tongue may sometimes cause you to bite off more than you can chew, especially when dealing with the king of the jungle. Students will enjoy describing how modern idioms can sometimes add humor to a story.

Yolen, Jane. *Where Have the Unicorns Gone?* Simon and Schuster, 2000.
Hardcover (LB): ISBN 0-689-82465-3.

Jane Yolen's story of the disappearance of the mythical unicorn is a metaphor for all the wild things that have vanished as a result of civilization's advance. Yet, despite the gloomy record, Yolen still holds out the glimmer of a chance for redemption. Ruth Sanderson's oils on Masonite panels add dimension to a beautifully written, flowing tale for older listeners. This has become one of my favorite picture books. (YA)

Young, Ed. *Voices of the Heart.* Scholastic, 1997. Hardcover (LB): ISBN 0-590-50199-2.
Based on 26 Chinese characters, each describing a feeling, this richly illustrated text uses layers of meaning to discover the depth of emotion behind each symbol. This would be a fine piece to use to discuss values and ethics in different cultures. The art in this book is thoughtful and striking. The text creates harmony with the words and pictures and invites readers to explore a full range of emotions about the very words that try to describe the depth of our feelings. (YA)

No longer just a first stage toward serious reading, the picture book is now enhancing math concepts, history lessons, art projects, science experiments, human relations development, and of course, the language arts program. Creative teachers have found ways to use picture books in all grade levels and in all subject areas.
—Susan Hall, *Using Picture Storybooks To Teach Literary Devices: Volume Two*

Sentence Fluency

Rhythm and cadence
Language with a beat
Variety and spice

Andrews Edwards, Julie, and Hamilton, Emma Walton. ***Simeon's Gift.*** HarperCollins, 2003. Hardcover (LB): ISBN 0-375-92567-8.

A new book by celebrity Julie Andrews and her daughter Emma, *Simeon's Gift* is a story about a search for knowledge and the discovery of true happiness. Minstrel Simeon risks everything in his quest to improve his mind and his music, but he eventually realizes that true happiness comes from caring and giving. A lyrical story written and beautifully illustrated in a style that adds to the atmosphere of the Renaissance that suffuses each page. An added bonus is the CD read by Julie Andrews. (YA)

Angelou, Maya. ***My Painted House, My Friendly Chicken, and Me.*** Crown, 2003. Hardcover (LB): ISBN 0-375-92567-8.

Eight-year-old Thandi, narrator of this delightful tale, will touch your heart and awaken your sense of vocal rhythm as she leads you on a visual and verbal tour of her native village. Wonderfully original sentence patterns sing across the pages: "I wonder, are little brothers in your village as mischievous as my little brother?" A delightful blend of text and photographic illustration gives the book a kind of personal portfolio feel. Adults and children alike will enjoy the playful variations in font size and style that help carry meaning in simple, yet effective ways. Like a good photo album, this book is a joy to read again and again.

Arro, Lena. ***Good Night, Animals.*** R & S Books, 2002. Hardcover: ISBN 91-29-65654-0.

Bubble and Pearl are set for an exciting adventure—sleeping in a tent. But a tent makes an attractive shelter for other creatures, too. And pretty soon they have a tent full of friends. The rhythmic prose of this story will have younger readers wanting to add to the list of camping guests.

Baker, Keith. ***Cat Tricks.*** Harcourt, 1997. Hardcover (LB): ISBN 0-15-292857-X.

A cleverly constructed book of sentence patterns, this book contains a surprise each time you turn the page. Sure to fire the imagination of younger readers.

Base, Graeme. ***The Sign of the Seahorse.*** Bt Bound, 1999. Hardcover (LB): ISBN 0-613-08755-0.

Adventure in and under the high seas is brought to dramatic reality through the inimitable imagination and vision of Graeme Base *(Animalia, The Eleventh Hour)*. You can spend hours just with the illustrations, then take another run through to enjoy the remarkable text. Wonderfully rhythmic, but equally appropriate for word choice and voice.

Baylor, Byrd. *The Table Where Rich People Sit.* Bt Bound, 1999.
Hardcover (LB): ISBN 0-613-08861-1.

Mountain Girl knows the family isn't rich, but like many young people, she misses the goodies that a little extra cash can buy. So, she calls a family meeting at the homemade kitchen table to discuss her feelings about their lack of money and the "stuff" that goes with it. However, after she lays out her case, her parents begin to help her see and appreciate the many riches that they have—the feel of the wind, the smell of the rain, the sound of the coyotes, the sight of the eagles. Gradually, Mountain Girl comes to appreciate how very rich she is. As with all of Byrd Baylor's books, it is so beautifully written that the rhythm and cadence are almost poetic. Her words sing to you as the thoughts invade your own world and you find yourself sitting at the very same table taking note of all the things that make your life worth living.

Bogan, Paulette. *Goodnight Lulu.* Bloomsbury, 2003. Hardcover: ISBN 1-58234-803-0.

Like youngsters everywhere, Lulu needs reassurance that the dark around her bed contains no bears, tigers, or alligators. But pigs? Momma chicken rises resourcefully to the test, and puts even that question to rest.

Bunting, Eve. *Anna's Table.* Northwold Books, 2003. Hardcover: ISBN 1-55971-841-2.

Anna's gift of a table is a door into the natural world. From a dead fiddler crab to the delicate bodies of a drift of butterflies, Anna is gently introduced to the cycle of life and the beauty in nature. The poetic form and colorful illustrations give this book a lyrical quality.

Burleigh, Robert. *Hoops.* Silver Whistle (Harcourt Brace), 1997.
Hardcover (LB): ISBN 0-15-201450-0.

How do I describe this book and do it justice? Perhaps the first few lines say enough. "Hoops. The game. Feel it. The rough roundness. The ball like a piece of the thin long reach of your body. The way it answers whenever you call. The never-stop back and forth flow, like tides going in, going out." And so it begins, a book about how it FEELS to play basketball from the inside out. This book is a sensation. I have read it a dozen times and on each reading I fall more in love with the idea, the rhythm, and the use of the cadence of language to mirror the feel of the basketball and the game. Kids love it; adults love it; it should be in every teacher's collection. A 100 percent guaranteed hit! (YA)

Cisneros, Sandra. *Hairs, Pelitos.* Apple Soup, 1994. Paperback: ISBN 0-679-89007-6.

The House on Mango Street is one of those books you keep buying and buying because each time you get a copy, you wind up giving it to someone else to enjoy. It's impossible not to share the engaging, lively, thoughtful, delicious, colorful, and exquisite collection of stories. Now comes the picture book of one of the chapters, "Hairs, Pelitos," so even young children can have access to Sandra Cisneros' beautiful thoughts and language. Use the original text and picture book as complements, or treasure this illustrated piece from the original. But whatever you do, don't miss them. Really.

Cummings, Pat. *Angel Baby.* Lothrop, Lee, & Shepard, 2000.
Hardcover (LB): ISBN 0-688-14822-0.

It is quite hard to know who the "angel" is in this clever, tongue-in-cheek account of a day in the life of Amanda Lynne and her baby brother. The poetic and rhyming style of the story add a dimension to the naughty antics of the baby, and help contrast his behavior to the "what an angel he can be" comment from Mom. And the ending will bring an extra chuckle. Also good for organization.

Dorros, Arthur. *Isla.* Bt Bound, 1999. Hardcover (LB): ISBN 0-613-14865-7.

"Hay mucho mas que ver," Abuela says to her granddaughter Rosalba. Indeed, there are many more places to see and explore in this English text, which is sprinkled with Spanish phrases. The two pick up their adventures from the earlier award-winning story, *Abuela,* as they visit places like the rain forest, an old market, and the harbor. This is a loving story that honors family and culture.

Erdrich, Louise. *The Range Eternal.* Hyperion Books, 2002. Hardcover: ISBN 0-7868-0220-0.

The Range Eternal, an old-fashioned stove, is the heart of a young girl's home, providing warmth, hot soup, and even comfort when icy monsters come calling. But the range is lost when electricity finally comes to the remote mountains, and with it goes a powerful symbol of a way of life. Can it be recaptured in the modern city? This is a lyrical story about a changing world, and the things that create a sense of home. (YA)

Esckelson, Laura. *The Copper Braid of Shannon O'Shea.* Dutton, 2003.
Hardcover (LB): ISBN 0-525-46138-8.

A troupe of sprites take on the task of unbraiding Shannon's coppery hair, but little do they suspect what they will find. From a piece of straw to a small island called "Atlantis," the discoveries are astonishing. A humorous tale in poetic form that invites an imaginative response from young listeners.

Fox, Mem. *Harriet, You'll Drive Me Wild!* Harcourt, 2000. Paperback: ISBN 0-15-201977-4.

Harriet Harris doesn't mean to create problems, but trouble just seems to be her constant companion. Eventually both she and her mother discover that love and a sense of humor can overcome even the most persistent irritations.

Fox, Mem. *Time for Bed.* Gulliver Books, 1993. Hardcover: ISBN 0-15-288183-2.

A beautiful way to say goodnight, these tender passages create a snuggly, content, end-of-the-day mood. The rhythm is gentle, but strong, and large print allows beginning readers to follow along. Just two lines to the page. Here's one to read aloud over and over. A fine book for illustrating how rhyme affects rhythm.

Fox, Mem. *Wombat Divine.* Harcourt Brace, 1995. Hardcover (LB): ISBN 0-15-201416-0.
This book cries out to be read aloud. Its phrasing is absolutely perfect to complement the story line. It would make a terrific group read piece, divided into parts, with the delightful line at the end, "You were divine, Wombat!" as the final crescendo. This story speaks to us all during those moments of wanting to fit in, but not knowing quite how. Wombat lives this experience as he tries to join in on the nativity play. No part is quite right for him until finally, the group realizes he would be the perfect Baby Jesus. You'll love this simple, yet poetic piece. Mem, you've done it again!

Gray, Libba Moore. *My Mama Had a Dancing Heart.* Orchard Books, 1995.
Hardcover: ISBN 0-531-08770-0.
The title alone on this one captured my attention. It is an indication of the lyrical text that follows in this delightful piece that celebrates the relationship of a mother and daughter who go through life living each moment and finding the joy in each season. Beautifully illustrated, each page is written like the lyrics of a song; a joyful ballet that is bursting with life and love.

Greenberg, David. *Slugs.* Little Brown, 1983. Hardcover: ISBN 0316-32658-5.
You don't have to be from the Oregon coast to enjoy this snappy story-poem about slugs. Kids of all ages will enjoy the mildly repulsive playfulness of Greenberg's prose. Notice how the sharp, succinct phrasing grows longer page by page until at the end it a-l-m-o-s-t stretches into complete sentences. Good for word choice, too.

Haseley, Dennis. *A Story for Bear.* Silver Whistle, 2002. Hardcover: ISBN 0-15-2002-391.
A young bear finds a piece of paper that leads him to develop a touching friendship with a woman who spends her summers alone in the woods. She reads aloud to him each day, and while not understanding the words, he is enchanted by the variety of sounds and emotions that her words produce in him. But what will happen to him during the long cold winter when she returns to her own world? An engrossing story about friendship, and the value of reading aloud. (YA)

Herron, Carolivia. *Nappy Hair.* Knopf, 1997. Hardcover (LB): ISBN 0-679-97937-9.
The inside jacket says it best: "While it seems that the family is poking fun at Brenda's hair, the nappiest, the curliest, the twistiest hair in the whole family, in fact they're admiring it by uncovering its meaning, its strength, its African-ness. The African American tradition of call-and-response makes *Nappy Hair* a story for many voices. As the dialogue builds, its spirit draws you in, rolls you around, and doesn't let you go. Finally, its blues rhythms slow down and let you off at the end." And this from a high school teacher in South Carolina:
"It is my opinion that using novels about blacks or written by African American writers in classrooms will help clear up any misconceptions, stereotypes, and myths about African Americans. If teachers would use more multicultural books in their classrooms, it would enable children to understand and respect the diversity of other cultures. It is a must if we want the world to be a better place in which to live."—A black woman and teacher

Howitt, Mary. ***The Spider and the Fly.*** Simon & Schuster, 2002.
Hardcover (LB): ISBN 0-689-85289-4.
> This is a beautifully rewritten and illustrated version of Mary Howitt's poem. The black and white format adds to the dramatic, ghoulish atmosphere of the story, that has as much relevance today as it did when it first appeared in 1829. A wonderful production that has joined my collection. (YA)

Ireland, Karin. ***Don't Take Your Snake for a Stroll.*** Harcourt, 2003.
Hardcover (LB): ISBN 0-15-202361-5.
> A message for pet owners: Pets belong at home, not in the mall or at the swing-dance party! A humorous look at what could go wrong if the wrong animal gets into the wrong situation at the wrong time. Don't say you were not warned.

Kay, Verla. ***Homespun Sarah.*** G.P. Putnam, 2003. Hardcover: ISBN 0-399-23417-9.
> This is the story of everyday life in the 1700s, with Sarah in need of a new dress, to be made, of course, from homespun cloth. A wonderfully poetic rendition of a moment in history.

Lawrence, Jacob. ***The Great Migration: An American Story.*** Bt Bound, 1999.
Hardcover (LB): ISBN 0-785-77628-1.
> "To me, migration means movement. There was conflict and struggle. But out of the struggle came a kind of poetry and even beauty. 'And the migrants kept coming' is a refrain of triumph over adversity. If it rings true for you today, then it must still strike a chord in our American experience." This majestic work of 60 sequential paintings by the African American artist eloquently tells the story of the southern black migration to the northern workplace and a new way of life in the 1920s. The fluency and movement from picture to picture underscore the theme of a culture in transition. Don't miss this book—it is thoughtful and powerful. (Also use for organization and voice.)

Lee, Ho Baek. ***While We Were Out.*** Kane Miller, 2003. Hardcover: ISBN 1-929132-44-1.
> The secret lives of rabbits is anything but dull if we are to believe this tale! An open door provides access to all kinds of exciting activities for a little bunny left on his own all day. You will never think about your pet in quite the same way after reading this cleverly constructed story. Younger listeners will delight in the ending.

Lester, Helen. ***Something Might Happen.*** Houghton Mifflin, 2003.
Hardcover (LB): ISBN 0-6182-5406-4.
> Twitchly the lemur is so afraid of doing anything—even going to the 4th of February parade—that he does nothing except sit and be afraid, until the day Aunt Fidget drops by. Then in one sweeping visit Twitchly becomes a new person. A story to encourage youngsters to risk trying something new. Also good for word choice.

Lithgow, John. ***I'm a Manatee.*** Simon and Schuster, 2003. Hardcover (LB): ISBN 0-689-85427-7.
> This wondrous story is of a boy who dreams of being … a manatee. Written in poetic form (and including a sing-a-long CD), the story takes us into the underwater world of probably the ugliest creature on this planet. A colorful tale with a tongue-in-cheek message. Also good for word choice.

Livingston, Irene. *Finklehopper Frog.* Tricycle Press, 2003. Hardcover: ISBN 1-58246-075-2.
Finklehopper Frog wants to join the jogging crowd, but his choice of running suit and natural tendency to hopping keep him out of the mainstream. Until, that is, a fellow hopper lets him know that it's OK to just be yourself. A great way to send the message that we each bop to our own drummer. Also excellent for the traits of word choice and ideas.

Long, Melinda. *How I Became a Pirate.* Harcourt, 2003. Hardcover: ISBN 0-15-201848-4.
Jeremy Jacob wants to be a pirate. But true to the moral "be careful what you wish for," he soon finds out that life on a pirate galleon entails some sacrifice—like bedtime stories. Jeremy, however, falls on his feet when the pirates find they need a "digger" to bury their treasure. A humorous look at wishful thinking. Also good for word choice.

Lundgren, Mary Beth. *Seven Scary Monsters.* Clarion, 2003.
Hardcover (LB): ISBN 0-395-88913-8.
This counting book is full of monsters who one-by-one are eliminated until there are none. But then there is no fun, or noise, or company. Youngsters will enjoy the colorful illustrations and the rhythmic style of this story.

Lyons, Dana. *The Tree.* Illumination Arts, 2002. Hardcover ISBN 0-9701907-3-5.
This wonderfully lyrical and beautifully illustrated book makes the case for preserving our remaining old-growth forests. *The Tree* is the song of an ancient Douglas Fir rooted in the rainforest of the Pacific Northwest, but it sings of the danger to all wild things that is posed by the thoughtless destruction of the environment by humankind. A lesson for all ages. Good for ideas, too! (YA)

Many, Paul. *The Great Pancake Escape.* Walker, 2002. Hardcover (LB): ISBN 0-8027-8796-7.
Here's a case of renegade pancakes on the rampage! Dad's attempt at cooking breakfast goes all wrong when he uses the wrong cookbook to mix up the batter. And the kids are left to track down the elusive hotcakes, or miss out on the most important meal of the day. This poetic story can be read or sung aloud. Also good for word choice.

McCarty, Peter. *Little Bunny on the Move.* Henry Holt, 1999. Hardcover: ISBN 0-8050-4620-8.
"A bunny goes where a bunny must," and with that message the little creature just keeps going. Young readers will appreciate the single-mindedness of this little guy as he refuses to be distracted from his mission—to get home.

McLerran, Alice. *The Ghost Dance.* Clarion Books (Houghton Mifflin), 1995.
Hardcover (LB): ISBN 0-395-63168-8.
Whenever I pack for a workshop, I sort through all my picture books. Then I re-sort, and finally go through them one last time, trying to create a balance between what I know teachers will love and what my back and luggage can withstand. This book will always make the cut—ALWAYS. Not only is the example included for a lesson on fluency, but I find it so moving that I get emotional every time I read it to myself or to a group of adults or kids. Its message of cultural harmony from the tradition of the Paiute Indians is beautifully told, but doesn't preach. It's so simple. We can learn from each other, which allows us to move to a better place TOGETHER.

Muth, John. ***Stone Soup.*** Scholastic, 2003. Hardcover: ISBN 0-439-33909-X.
    In this retelling of the familiar traditional story, the setting is China. A trio of monks decides that a little trickery is all that is needed to encourage villagers to show a more neighborly attitude to each other. This is a lyrically written and beautifully illustrated version of the story that captures the atmosphere of the time and the place. (YA)

Myers, Walter Dean. ***Harlem.*** Scholastic, 1997. Hardcover: ISBN 0-590-54340-7.
    A richly illustrated copy of Walter Dean Myers's glorious poem, this piece cries out to be read aloud. It's a chorus of rich sounds and life connections telling the tale of an important piece of American culture. "Come, take a journey on the 'A' train that started on the banks of the Niger and has not ended." Take the journey of *Harlem.* (YA)

Panzer, Nora, Ed. ***Celebrate America in Poetry and Art.*** Hyperion Books in association with the National Museum of Art, Smithsonian Institution, 1994. Hardcover: ISBN 1-56282-664-6.
    Beautiful scarcely begins to cover it. Within these pages lie some of the finest of American art and verse, and editor Nora Panzer has done a marvelous job of coordinating art with text to create a special sense of time, place, or mood on every page. This is a tour of America not to be missed. This fine book is incredible for Fluency. (YA)

Paulsen, Gary. ***Dogteam.*** Bt Bound, 1999. Hardcover (LB): ISBN 0-785-77932-9.
    Into the magic of a moonlit winter night, the dogs who love to run, the dogs Gary Paulsen knows so well, take their owner—and you, the reader—on a star-spangled journey "away from camp, away from people, away from houses and light and noise and into only one thing, into only winternight …." Live the magic, the speed, the thrill of running, the chilly encounter with wolves, the beauty of the night woods, and the warmth of coming home at the end of the run. A book that transports readers in time and place. Ruth Wright Paulsen's remarkable illustrations are so right for Gary Paulsen's text that the two seem to come from one mind and heart. Only a writer with a true love of the woods and dog sledding could have packed such power into his work. The text sings like blades along the snow. Is it prose or poetry? Does it matter? Either way, it will pull you into the blue world of winternight.

Paulsen, Gary. ***Work Song.*** Harcourt Brace, 1997. Hardcover: ISBN 0-15-200980-9.
    Here's a real treasure. This nonfiction work from Gary Paulsen and his illustrator wife, Ruth Wright Paulsen, could be used in lots of ways. The text honors the many different jobs that we have in the world of work—interestingly juxtaposed one to the next through the pages. Along with illustrations that tend to obscure the male/female role (who can tell the gender of a person inside a diving suit or a welder's helmet, for instance), the text flows simply and beautifully from beginning to end. "It is keening noise and jolting sights, and hammers flashing in the light, and houses up and trees in sun, and trucks on one more nighttime run …." Can you feel it? I feel a sense of honor in this piece. It is good to work—with your hands or in an office—the WORK is good. (YA)

Perry, Robert. *Down at the Seaweed Café.* Raincoast Books, 2003.
Hardcover: ISBN 1-5519-2473-0.
> The Seaweed Café is the place to hear salty tales of Spanish shipwrecks, jumping whales, and giant cadborosaurus. And the invitation is always there to sing and dance as well. A great place to spend a few imaginative hours. Also good for word choice.

Preston, Tim. *The Lonely Scarecrow.* Dutton, 1999. Hardcover: ISBN 0-525-46080-2.
> Scarecrow wishes more than anything else that birds and animals would be his friends, but through the spring, summer, and fall they all keep their distance. In winter, when scarecrow's features are masked by glistening snow, the animals are ready to give him a chance. But will it last when the snow is gone? An engaging story of friendship and acceptance.

Reiss, Mike. *Late for School.* Peachtree Publishers, 2003. Hardcover: ISBN 1-56145-286-6.
> Smitty's route to school is just full of improbable obstacles that all seem designed to make him late, a circumstance he finds unacceptable. But when he finally arrives, why is the school locked up and empty? Wonderful illustrations turn this poetic story into a great adventure. Also good for the trait of presentation.

Say, Allen. *A River Dream.* Houghton Mifflin, 1988. Hardcover (LB): ISBN 0-395-48294-1.
> Allen Say has a magical touch. In this story he brings his love of nature and the environment into play while spinning his story web characterizing a young boy's journey toward maturity. His words are soft and gentle and the rhythm of the piece rocks you into a cradle of sweetness. The questions young Mark faces are universal; what is unique about Allen Say's writing is the honesty and sincerity that permeate each line, each carefully worded phrase.

Shange, Ntozake, and Bearden, Romare. *I Live in Music.* Welcome Enterprises, 1999.
Hardcover: ISBN 0-9418-0709-6.
> "Shange's lyrical poem is a tribute to the language of music and the magical, often mystical rhythms that connect people. Music defines who we are as individuals, the places where we live, and how we exist within our communities. Music is life." This poem has a syncopated style and melody all its own. Looking for a book to help students develop an ear for the rhythm and flow of words? This is it! As beautifully illustrated as it is written.

Siebert, Diane. *Heartland.* Bt Bound, 1999. Hardcover (LB): ISBN 0-833-59080-4.
> For our many friends in the heartland, this piece, written in rhyming poetry, celebrates your beautiful countryside and way of life. The reader experiences the rich majesty of the Midwest farmland—a land where nature rules everyday life and man has learned to live gracefully with her power. (YA)

Steig, Jeanne. *Consider the Lemming.* Bt Bound, 1999. Hardcover (LB): ISBN 0-374-41361-4.
(Out of print)
> "All the appeal of Ogden Nash at his best. There are limericks here that may prove immortal." —*Kirkus Reviews.*
>
> All the whimsical fun of William Steig's illustrations are combined with Jeanne Steig's wacky text. Unpredictable and zany, with insight and perspective to make you chuckle.

Thayer, Ernest L. *Casey at the Bat: A Ballad of the Republic Sung in the Year 1888.*
Simon & Schuster, 2003. Hardcover: ISBN 0-689-85494-3.

> The 1888 poem is beautifully brought back to life by powerful illustrations that capture all the tension and excitement of a close baseball game. This book provides a great opportunity for a new generation of young fans to enjoy the story and connect with the inimitable characters. (YA)

Viorst, Judith. *Alexander y el Dia Terrible, Horrible, Espantoso, Horroroso.* Atheneum, 1989.
Hardcover (LB): ISBN 0-689-31591-0.

> Kids and adults alike relate to the chain of horrible events chronicled in this classic story. For students learning English as a second language, the trait of Fluency is one of the most difficult. Read this Spanish version, or whichever language version best suits your students' needs, and listen to the rhythm and flow of the text. In all languages, this piece just works! (For English version, see Page 36.)

Viorst, Judith. *If I Were in Charge of the World, and Other Worries.* Bt Bound, 1999.
Hardcover (LB): ISBN 0-808-55022-5.

> If you've ever had trouble apologizing or keeping a secret, had a crush or a broken heart, there's a poem here for you. Written with humor and understanding, Viorst's poems are certain to delight children and adults alike. As you read them, be aware of the cadence and rhythm that moves ideas along and delights the tongue! Students will enjoy adding their own personal reflections on life to this rich treasure of poetry.

Viorst, Judith. *My Mama Says There Aren't Any Zombies, Ghosts, Vampires, Creatures, Demons, Monsters, Fiends, Goblins, or Things.* Bt Bound, 1999.
Hardcover (LB): ISBN 0-808-52518-2.

> "How can Nick believe his mother's telling him there aren't any monsters when she forgets what his favorite flavor of ice cream is? Or when she makes him wear boots and it doesn't even rain? Well, sometimes mamas DO make mistakes … but sometimes they don't." This story invites oral reading and page turning.

Willard, Nancy. *A Visit to William Blake's Inn: Poems for the Innocent and Experienced Travelers.* Harcourt Brace, 1981. Hardcover (LB): ISBN 0-15-293822-2.

> Inspired by the poems of William Blake, Nancy Willard has written a book of magical poems about life at an imaginary inn, run by none other than William Blake himself. The inn is staffed by two mighty dragons that brew and bake, two angels that wash and shake the featherbeds, and a rabbit who shows visitors to their rooms. The incredible illustrations reflect an appreciation and understanding of life in London 200 years ago. (Newbery Medal and Caldecott Honor award winner)

Like fine poetry, children's picture books are meant to be seen and heard. Even adolescents like to be read to …. By reading aloud I not only let kids hear the richness of the language, but I invite adolescents to read them also.
—Linda Reif, *Beyond Words: Picture Books for Older Readers and Writers*

Conventions

Simple and complex editorial skills
Consistency and accuracy
Making reading simple and interesting

Petty, Kate. *The Amazing Pop-Up Grammar Book.* Dutton (Penguin), 1996.
Hardcover: ISBN 0-525-45580-9.

The title pretty much covers it—a POP-UP grammar book. How amazing! This is a delightful collection of little tips on nouns, verbs, adjectives, adverbs, prepositions, conjunctions, plurals, possessives, some punctuation practice and, finally, sentence tricks. Little flaps, pull-open windows, matching flaps, and so forth fill this piece. When I put this book out at workshops, teachers pore over it and cry out in delighted surprise at the clever little grammar activities. In fact, they wore out one copy and I'm on my second one already. I bet your students will enjoy it just as much.

Prelutsky, Jack. *Hooray for Diffendoofer Day.* Alfred A. Knopf, 1998.
Hardcover (LB): ISBN 0-679-99008-9.

Dr. Seuss's last book, lovingly completed by Jack Prelutsky, is a tribute to every classroom teacher who believes that education is more about thinking than facts. The staff and students at Diffendoofer School are concerned when they find out they are going to be tested. But Miss Bonkers is sure that her students will do OK because, "We've taught you how to think." Begun before 1991, this book is an insightful commentary on the current push for standards and testing. It also contains a wonderful section on how the book was made, with original illustrations that include revision and editing notes; a great resource for trait instruction.

Wheeler, Lisa. *Old Cricket.* Atheneum, 2003. Hardcover: ISBN 0-689-84510-3.

A creak in his knee, a crick in his neck, and a crack in his back give Old Cricket all the excuses he needs to get out of fixing his roof (he's no dumb bug). But Old Crow (he's no birdbrain) causes a change in Old Cricket's plans, and he ends up fixing it anyway. A funny story that is enhanced by glorious illustrations.

The students lean forward in their seats, all eyes on the reader and book. As the reader holds up the pictures, or walks around the room holding the pages toward them, they shift around in their chairs to get a better view. When the reader lowers her voice to a near whisper, they strain to hear every word. As they listen, they respond—sometimes with a thoughtful silence, sometimes even with tears. The book is 32 pages long, and its text is so brief it can be read in its entirety in about 10 minutes .... Elementary school? First grade, perhaps? No, this is a university class ... good picture books can be enjoyed by people of all ages.

—Rudine Simms Bishop and Janet Hickman, *Beyond Words: Picture Books for Older Readers and Writers*

Presentation

The form and presentation of the text enhances the ability
for the reader to understand and connect with the message.
It is pleasing to the eye.

Avi. ***Silent Movie.*** Atheneum, 2003. Hardcover: ISBN 0-689-84145-0.
The exciting story of a family newly arrived in the United States from Europe in the late 19th century, this book is written and illustrated to create the feel of a silent movie. Staccato text matched with black and white line drawings effectively capture the tone and atmosphere of those old Charlie Chaplin and Buster Keaton films. A book designed not only to entertain, but to encourage an interest among older readers in an intriguing art form. (YA)

Devine, Barbara. ***Elvis the Camel.*** Stacey International, 2002. Hardcover: ISBN 1-900988-39-9.
A camel is named "Elvis"? You'll understand how this unlikely association comes about in this simple story of friendship and compassion set in the sun and sand of the Middle East. The illustrations by Patricia Al Fakhri eloquently capture the atmosphere of this ancient dry land.

Goble, Paul. ***Mystic Horse.*** HarperCollins. 2003. Hardcover: ISBN 0-06-029814-6.
The extraordinary illustrations of this book are matched by an engrossing story based on Pawnee legend. An old, decrepit horse turns into a magnificent war steed only to be killed as a result of his rider's betrayal. Is it possible to forgive such a mistake? Paul Goble is the Caldecott Medal-winning author of *The Girl Who loved Wild Horses.* (YA)

Kirk, David. ***Miss Spider's Tea Party.*** Scholastic, 1996. Hardcover: ISBN 0-590-69782-X.
No one, it seems, is prepared to give Miss Spider any time, even though she is only inviting them to tea (can you wonder, after the fly's fate?). But then, one bedraggled moth spreads the story of her kindness, and the story changes. A beautifully illustrated book that may be used as a counting book for younger listeners.

Martin, Jacqueline Briggs. ***Snowflake Bentley.*** Houghton Mifflin, 1998.
Hardcover (LB): ISBN 0-395-86162-4.
A story of courage, determination, and vision, Snowflake Bentley recounts the life story of W.A. Bentley, a pioneer in the scientific study of snow and ice. Starting with his youthful attempts at keeping them from melting long enough to draw, to his untimely death after a snowstorm, Bentley's fascination with snow was unwavering. Jacqueline Martin's lyrical writing is given an old-world feel by the hand-colored woodcuts of Mary Azarian. (A Caldecott Medal winner; YA)

Muth, Jon J. ***The Three Questions.*** Scholastic, 2002. Hardcover (LB): ISBN 0-439-19996-4.
When is the best time to do things? Who is the most important one? What is the right thing to do? Nicolai searches among his friends for the answers to his questions, but finds them in his own actions. A thought-provoking, wonderfully illustrated book that will provide lots of talking points for readers and listeners of all ages. Also good for ideas. (YA)

Waldman, Neil. ***The Starry Night.*** Boyds Mills Press, 1999. Hardcover (LB): ISBN 1-56397-736-2.
How would New York look through the eyes and brush of Vincent Van Gogh? Join Bernard on a journey of discovery into the art world of the great Dutch painter, and see the city from a fresh new perspective. An effective integration of art and literature. (YA)

Wiesner, David. ***Three Little Pigs.*** Clarion, 2001. Hardcover: ISBN 0-618-00701-6.
The three little pigs survive the wolf's onslaught by getting "out of the story" and enlisting the aid of a similarly displaced dragon. But then it is time to teach the wolf a lesson, so it is back to the story, and a happy ending. This cleverly-constructed book was awarded the Caldecott Medal.

Wilson, Gina. ***Ignis.*** Candlestick Press, 2003. Hardcover: ISBN 0-7636-1623-0.
Ignis is the star of the young dragons, able to fly higher and faster than any of his companions. But Ignis is not able to breathe fire. He goes in search of this important skill and only meets with success when he climbs alone to the top of a volcano. A well-written and beautifully illustrated tale of an individual in search of himself. Also great for the traits of ideas and sentence fluency.

I roam the classics through a forest of treasures
and love their elegant balance of style and substance.
Inspired, I lay down the book I was reading
and let words pour out from my brush.
—Lu Ji, *The Art of Writing*

Teaching Lessons and Activities

The next section of the 2004 *Picture Books* bibliography contains more than 50 new lessons to assist you in planning to integrate the six traits and picture books into your classroom curriculum. Thank you so very, very much to teachers from New Jersey to Washington, from South Carolina to California, for your many contributions and ideas. On the following pages, you'll find a full range of practical, ready-to-use ideas for classrooms K–14 and beyond, organized by trait. Perhaps you'll want to use the lessons exactly as they are described; or, even better, maybe you'll get an idea from one or more of the suggestions and come up with wonderful new ideas of your own.

You know how much writing is influenced by reading and vice versa. Here is a place for all our students to get some real, hands-on experience with the power of the writing/reading connection. Enjoy!

"Since I've started using picture books with my students, they really understand about clear ideas and the different ways they could be organized in their writing. And their voices … WOW! The models in the picture books have given my students courage to be writers themselves and the improvement in the quality of their work overall is absolutely amazing."
—A ninth-grade teacher in Kent, Washington

Ideas

- Make a list of things to write about from ideas found in picture books.

- Compare the way two authors write about the same Idea.

- Count the number of words in the average picture book and discuss how long it really takes to tell a story or explain an Idea well.

- List topics that seem too big, trite, or overused and look for ways authors of picture books have handled these topics well.

- Select a topic from a content-area class and create a picture book to teach someone else what has been learned.

- Keep a writer's notebook of potential writing topics found in picture books.

Ideas Activity 1

Book: *Alphabet City* by Stephen T. Johnson

Grades: All

Time Required: Varies—at least one to two hours recommended (easily broken into shorter segments if more convenient)

Materials/Preparation:
1. A copy of the book
2. Colored overhead transparencies of a few pages to show the illustrator's use of graphic design
3. Drawing/painting/sketching materials

What To Do:
1. Read the book aloud.
2. Discuss students' reactions. What was the author trying to do with this text? Did he succeed? Which letters did students like best? Which did they find the most unusual? What different artistic treatments did they see represented?
3. Ask students to look around the room and describe any letter shapes they find. Which ones were easy? Which ones took a little more time to notice? Make a list, or draw pictures of what they discover.
4. Visit other places in the school—playground, cafeteria, gym, hallways, media center, main office, and so forth. As students find examples of letters, ask them to sketch the letters as close to the original as they can, paying close attention to their color, texture, location, and the context in which they were found.
5. Encourage students to look for other things, too, like numbers, letter combinations, and so forth. If you can, take students out of the school to parks, museums, big streets, stores, and so forth, so they can find shapes and letters in their natural context.
6. If you have access to several student-friendly cameras, have students take pictures of the letters and/or numbers as they are discovered so the complete drawings or paintings can be done later.
7. Have students decide whether they would like to make their own alphabet books, a display, or some other product from their research.
8. Display final work in the room, hallway, and other places around the school.

How Does This Activity Connect to the Trait of Ideas?
- Learning to observe carefully
- Looking beyond the obvious
- Noticing details someone else might not see
- Bringing your own interpretation to everyday objects

Ideas Activity 2

Book: *Whoever You Are* by Mem Fox

Grades: Third and fourth

Time Required: 45–60 minutes

Materials/Preparation:
1. A copy of the book
2. Pencils, pens, and paper

What To Do:
1. Discuss students' personal experiences with individuals they perceived as "different." Ask, "How or what did you feel?" Share an experience of your own.
2. Ask students to listen for the author's message as you read the book aloud.
3. Discuss the author's message and brainstorm the ways in which we are all alike, whoever we are.
4. Have each student write a letter to another student the same age, in a different country. Ask them to share a similarity and a difference: looks, schools, homes, countries, and so forth. Remind them that for that students to "see" what they are sharing, they must include juicy details that show, not tell, so the pictures the readers see will be clear. Ideal activity for pen pal classrooms if another classroom does the same activity. (Internet pen pals are available, too!)

How Does This Activity Connect to the Trait of Ideas?
- For the similarities and differences to be clear to the audience, authors must include details that create clear pictures thousands of miles away, around the world.
- When students use specific "showing" details, it helps readers understand the message of the piece.

Ideas Activity 3

Books: *Wilfrid Gordon McDonald Partridge* by Mem Fox
To Hell With Dying by Alice Walker

Grades: Middle school on up

Time Required: One week or until you feel satisfied

Materials/Preparation:
1. A copy of both books
2. Notebook for each student

What To Do:
1. Read both books aloud.
2. Let students react to ideas in each book in notebooks and in small-group discussions.
3. Ask: What kept your attention? What is really important about the topics? What did you gain as a reader?
4. After class discussion of how the ideas worked in each book, introduce the writing assignment:
   a) Compare and contrast the themes from the two books
   b) Compare and contrast elderly life and young life

How Does This Activity Connect to the Trait of Ideas?
- Picking two books that deal with the elderly provides an opportunity for students to see similar ideas written differently.
- Contrasting authors' treatments of a similar theme can illustrate how to focus an idea, shape it, add details, and make it your own.

Ideas Activity 4

Book: *What You Know First* by Patricia MacLachlan

Grades: All

Time Required: Two 30-minute sessions

Materials/Preparation:
1. A copy of the book
2. Pencils, pens, and paper
3. Three or four items of your own that remind you of your original home

What To Do:
1. Explain a proposed situation to students: Your parents tell you that in a month you are moving to another state because of a great job for one or both of the parents. (Choose a state that would be opposite or would be a big change for the students, e.g., from Washington state to Arizona.)
2. Have students make a quick list of things they would miss from their state.
3. Read the book aloud.
4. Show students the items you brought that remind you of your home/state and explain why you chose them.
5. Have students generate a list of things they would take that would represent and help them remember something from their home that they would miss. Have them write an explanation of their favorite three items.

How Does This Activity Connect to the Trait of Ideas?
- This lesson helps students go from the general—moving—to the specific. What would you take?
- Students focus on linking specific individual items to larger ideas and themes.
- Students learn that each piece of writing, though on the same or a similar topic, can turn out unique to the individual.

Ideas Activity 5

Book: *A Street Called Home* by Aminah Brenda Lynn Robinson

Grades: Intermediate

Time Required: Two to three days

Materials/Preparation:
1. A copy of the book
2. Colored pencils, pens, and paper

What To Do:
1. Discuss the people who make up your community, street, and neighborhood.
2. Direct the discussion to a more specific community—the school.
3. Read aloud different pages from the book.
4. List people who make up your school community.
5. Assign each student to a specific person in the school, e.g., principal, secretary, teacher, custodian, and so forth.
6. Have students interview their person. Set up interview appointments ahead of time.
7. Have students write interview questions and then a summary about their person.
8. Have students draw a picture and write a description.
9. Put it all together in a book to have in the front office or out for open house.

How Does This Activity Connect to the Trait of Ideas?
- Students generate ideas about the things that make up the world around us: our community and home.
- By focusing on one person from the school community, students concentrate their attention and add their own indepth piece to the larger piece created by the group.

Ideas Activity 6

Book: *The Old Woman Who Named Things* by Cynthia Rylant

Grades: Third through 12th

Time Required: 60 minutes

Materials/Preparation:
1. A copy of the book
2. Pencils, pens, and paper

What To Do:
1. Read the book aloud, but stop on Page 5: "The old woman never worried about outliving any of them, and her days were happy."
2. Discuss other objects the old woman could name.
3. Have students list items they own and have them give the objects names. Example: bike, bed, shoes, dresser, computer, and so forth
4. Have students share the names they chose and ask them why they chose a particular name. Have them write a short explanation about the name.
5. Have students select the best ideas and then write stories about their objects and how they came to be named. (Can also be used for a word choice lesson.)
6. Have students share their stories.

Additional Activity 1:
1. Continue reading the story, but stop on the bottom of Page 22 where it says, "Then he asked her what its name was."
2. Have students list names for the dog and explain why those were their choices. Show the picture of the puppy to the students. List attributes of the dog or those that are common to most dogs.
3. Have students pick one of the names and write a story about the dog, or continue the end of the story using the dog's name.

Additional Activity 2:
1. Show students the picture on Page 1 (woman standing on the porch looking outside), or Page 10 (old woman sitting in the red chair).
2. Have students write a description or story about this old woman. What does she see? What is she thinking? What has her life been like?

How Does This Activity Connect to the Trait of Ideas?
- Generating names like the old woman in the story gives students a starting point for ideas.
- The illustrations, captivating and rich with expression, create a starting point for ideas.

Ideas Activity 7

Book: *Amelia's Notebook* by Marissa Moss

Grades: Third through eighth

Time Required: 60 minutes

Materials/Preparation:
1. A copy of the book
2. Journal/notebook for each student
3. Pencils, pens, and paper
4. Copies of a few pages of the journal on transparencies or an opaque projector to show students examples of the pictures.

What To Do:
1. Read the book aloud.
2. Discuss a writer's notebook—mention that it can be about anything. It can even include pictures or taped- or glued-in items.
3. Show the first page of *Amelia's Notebook.*
4. Have students design the cover page for their personal writing notebook.

How Does This Activity Connect to the Trait of Ideas?
- This is a good example of a conglomeration of ideas. It shows students that a journal can be a fun way to record pictures and thoughts, and a way to write down ideas that can be the starting point for other stories or writing topics.
- See *A Writer's Notebook* by Ralph Fletcher for more ideas and connections to the trait of ideas.

Ideas Activity 8

Book: *My Mama Had a Dancing Heart* by Libba Moore Gray

Grades: Fourth through eighth

Time Required: 60 minutes

Materials/Preparation:
1. Pencils, pens, and paper
2. Glue and scissors

What To Do:
1. Read the book aloud.
2. Discuss the book, and think of other special things you do with your family that make time stand still for a precious moment.
3. Life is a celebration—brainstorm all the possible things we can do to celebrate things in life. Every day we should find one thing to illustrate and write about that has been a celebration.
4. Do one activity from the book in class. Let students enjoy and experience the activity and then write about it using descriptive words.
5. Link this book with *Celebrations* by Byrd Baylor and compare/contrast the books and their messages.

How Does This Activity Connect to the Trait of Ideas?
- Students help find everyday moments to celebrate.
- Students notice the things that make us happy—big and small.

Ideas Activity 9

Book: *The Table Where Rich People Sit* by Byrd Baylor

Grades: Fourth through eighth

Time Required: 20 minutes

Materials/Preparation:
1. A copy of the book
2. Other book or books with related themes, for example, *The Keeping Quilt*
3. Pencils, pens, and paper

What To Do:
1. Discuss what was important to this family. Discuss the importance of the family table.
2. Have students bring in one object that is a favorite "treasure" to them. (Share a treasure of yours, too!)
3. Have students draw a picture of a favorite activity their family does together and describe it.
4. Have students draw a place in their home where their families are most often together.
5. Share all these different special places.

How Does This Activity Connect to the Trait of Ideas?
- Exploring personal experiences as a source of ideas
- Connecting their lives to examples from literature
- Working with details on a focused topic

Organization

- Write the story to a wordless picture book and highlight the lead, transitional words, sequence patterns, and conclusion.

- Create a set of the best openings found in picture books.

- Create a set of the best conclusions found in picture books.

- Write a student-friendly set of guidelines for writing good openings and conclusions, based on what you find in picture books.

- Write a new ending to one or more picture books.

- Write a new picture book using the A–Z format on a topic from the current curriculum.

- Read and discuss the different organizational structures found in a sampling of books.

Organization Activity 1

Book: *Zoom* and *ReZoom* by Ivan Banyai

Grades: All

Time Required: 30–45 minutes

Materials/Preparation:
1. Two copies of each of the books.
2. Tear the pages out of one and laminate them. (Keep the other copy intact to use at the end of this sorting activity.)
3. Mix up all the laminated pictures so they are no longer in the original order.

What To Do:
1. Have students work as one large group (if you have one set of individual pages to the book) or smaller groups if you have several sets, and put the pages back in their original order.
2. Suggest students lay all the pages out so they can see the whole range before they try to sort.
3. Ask students to keep track of the kind of things that are influencing their decisions—color, format, layout, size, and so forth.
4. When students have finished sorting, discuss why they made the decisions they did. Ask why they picked some pictures for the beginning, and why they picked others for the ending. Ask them to explain the transitions they noticed in the middle—were some pictures used as a bridge to another sequence?
5. Discuss the similarities between the way they ordered the pictures and the way they would organize a piece of writing. Reinforce the notion of a good beginning that draws you in, a sense of resolution at the end that leaves you thinking, and the transitions that link ideas in the middle and move you through the text.
6. Ask students to hold up the pictures that they think were good transition pieces in the middle. Ask if there is anything in written composition that resembles what this artist has done to move us along through the sequence of drawings (hint: lead sentences in paragraphs). Discuss how important this is to strong organization in writing.
7. Try this with other wordless picture books. (See the bibliography under Organization for other titles.)

How Does This Activity Connect to the Trait of Organization?
- Figuring out where the beginning is and how to get the reader/viewer's attention
- Putting things in logical order—sequencing
- Deciding where the end is and how to clearly wrap it all up
- Observing the "flow" of a piece that is well organized and applying those techniques to their own writing or other original works

Organization Activity 2

Book: *The Frog Princess?* by Pamela Mann

Grades: Intermediate

Time Required: 30–60 minutes

Materials/Preparation:
1. A copy of the book
2. Other examples of children's fairy tales (see partial list at the end of this lesson)
3. Pencils, pens, and paper

What To Do:
1. Share with students one of your favorite fairy tales, but talk about what it would be like if the ending was different and unexpected. For example, what if Cinderella stayed with the prince after midnight and didn't care about being in rags, or what if she berated him about being superficial, or what if the prince actually married one of the stepsisters?
2. Read the book aloud. Discuss the surprise ending.
3. Have students write a familiar fairy tale but change the ending to the unexpected.

Additional Activity:
1. Read the book aloud, but stop after the prince kisses the frog.
2. Have students write a description of what the frog turns into after the kiss.
3. Share the examples.
4. Read the real ending.
5. Have students rework their ending to one that is unexpected.
6. Have students write a different familiar fairy tale but change the ending to the unexpected by changing one of the characters.

How Does This Activity Connect to the Trait of Organization?
- Using a familiar story, but then changing the ending in a unique way, creates a sense of how conclusions can make the familiar different
- Focusing on conclusions highlights how to wrap up a piece and leave the reader thinking about the message

Other Favorite Fairy Tale Titles:
The Frog Prince, Continued
Rumplestiltskin's Daughter
The True Story of the Three Little Pigs
The Jolly Postman
Sleeping Ugly

Organization Activity 3

Book: *The Storm* by Marc Harshman

Grades: Third through eighth

Time Required: One class period

Materials/Preparation:
1. A copy of the book
2. Typed, short descriptive excerpts from the book describing the storm (one set for each pair of students)

What To Do:
1. Give students the descriptive excerpts and encourage them to try to sequence the phrases and sentences describing the storm.
2. Let pairs of students compare the order of their story with others.
3. As a group, discuss the order of the piece as most people interpreted. Ask for sequencing words or transitional words that help the reader know the order.
4. Compare the combined class version to the original story. Discuss any similarities and differences. Do any of the differences change the original piece in a significant way?

How Does This Activity Connect to the Trait of Organization?
- Students practice sequencing skills by looking for transitions and logical connections throughout the story.
- Students learn the value of transitions and sequencing clues so the reader is led through the piece logically.

Organization Activity 4

Book: *The Seasons Sewn* by Ann Whitford Paul

Grades: All

Time Required: 30 minutes

Materials/Preparation:
1. A copy of the book
2. Pencils, pens, writing paper, and graph paper
3. Examples of a few quilt patterns on overhead transparencies

What To Do:
1. Read the book aloud. Show the quilt pattern examples as you read about each type.
2. Ask students how the book is organized.
3. List the items in the book that make up the different seasons. Ask students how each item is appropriate for the corresponding season.
4. Have the students add to the list for each season.
5. In small groups, have students pick one of the items, write about it, and then make a quilt square (if time and resources allow).
6. Have students share the item and the quilt square. Make a large class quilt from the individual squares.

Integration—Math:
Discuss the geometric shapes, patterns, colors, and repetition of a quilt square.

Integration—History/Social Studies:
Research one or more of the following topics: the history of the quilt, quilt patterns and their origins, the social implications of quilting on a culture, such as the Amish culture.

How Does This Activity Connect to the Trait of Organization?
- Writing can be organized in a variety of ways, and an overall theme helps the students see a way to organize information.
- The format of this book encourages students to see recurring themes as a prime organization structure.

Organization Activity 5

Book: *Purr ... Children's Book Illustrators Brag About Their Cats* edited by Michael J. Rosen

Grades: All

Time Required: 30–40 minutes

Materials/Preparation:
1. A copy of the book
2. Pencils, pens, and paper
3. Stuffed-animal cat or picture of a cat

What To Do:
1. Give a pair or small group of students access to a selected page that has an illustration and description of an author's cat.
2. Let them read the page and focus on how the author organizes the story and uses the picture as part of that organization.
3. After 5–10 minutes have the students switch pages.
4. Repeat the activity several times.
5. Discuss the variety of organization in the stories. This can be done in small groups or as a whole class with a master list generated.
6. Referring to the stuffed-animal cat or picture of a cat, have the students write a story about this cat, working on the trait of organization by using one of the structures they already identified or any new ones they may identify. They can create the cat's characteristics and personality and illustrate it in their own way.
7. Share the new pieces with the group.

How Does This Activity Connect to the Trait of Organization?
- Students can see how a variety of stories on the same topic are organized.
- Students can look at the different genres of writing selected by authors, all on the same subject—cats—and the different forms of organization associated with these modes (narrative, expository, persuasive, poetry).

Organization Activity 6

Book: *The Day I Swapped My Dad for Two Goldfish* by Neil Gaiman

Grades: Fourth on up

Time Required: 45–60 minutes

Materials/Preparation:
1. A copy of the book
2. Pencils, pens, and paper

What To Do:
1. Read the book aloud.
2. Have students map out all the "swaps" on a flow chart.
3. Have them design their own items and the people with whom they could swap. (It can be real people and situations or completely made up.)
4. Make a flow chart with the new items.
5. Have students write a new story based on the flow chart.
6. In teams, have students act out the new stories for the class.

How Does This Activity Connect to the Trait of Organization?
- This story sets a pattern for the students to follow.
- In this piece, the organization helps the ideas stand out.

Organization Activity 7

Book: *Clown* by Quentin Blake

Grades: Second through ninth

Time Required: 30 minutes

Materials/Preparation:
1. A copy of the book
2. Pencils, pens, and paper

What To Do:
1. Show students the story, but stop on Page 12 where the clown falls out of the tree.
2. Talk about the sequencing highlights the clown goes through in the story. How do the pictures help tell the story?
3. Give students an idea for the ending—e.g., have the clown find a loving home (like the original story), or join the circus and become famous.
4. Have students write or draw pictures that fill in the story. Have them draw and write their ending.

How Does This Activity Connect to the Trait of Organization?
- A story has a logical order. There are clues that help the reader follow the story. In *Clown,* students need to pay careful attention to the clues so they can see the sequencing that occurs.
- By taking the clown on different adventures and linking the actions together, students model sequencing and create stories that don't lose the reader because important facts/clues are missing.
- This activity helps students identify the beginning, middle, and end of a story, and link them all together.

Organization Activity 8

Book: *Antics!* by Catherine Hepworth

Grades: All

Time Required: 30–60 minutes

Materials/Preparation:
1. A copy of the book
2. Pencils, pens, and paper
3. Several examples of ABC books (check local elementary library for examples)

What To Do:
1. Show a couple of ABC books to students. Discuss the qualities of an ABC book (alphabet, order, beginning letter starts the word or the picture identifies the letter, anticipating the next letter, etc.).
2. Read the book aloud.
3. After a few examples, have students guess the next word with the corresponding letter. Ask students what they think she will use for the letter 'L.'
4. Define each word and how it relates to the picture.
5. Ask students what theme ties all the letter entries together.
6. Have students list topics they can write about. Example: dogs, bikes, a teacher, a grade they liked, and so forth.

Additional Activity:
Decide on a theme for a new ABC book. Each student can be responsible for a specific letter of the alphabet. Or, each student, pairs, or small groups can write all the ABCs about a topic the whole class agrees to use.

How Does This Activity Connect to the Trait of Organization?
ABC books are a natural selection for organization. The order of the alphabet gives the students a way to organize their thoughts and then put together a book.

Other ABC Books:
Alphabet City
Z Was Zapped
A Walk Through the Forest

Organization Activity 9

Book: *Two Bad Ants* by Chris Van Allsburg

Grades: Third on up

Time Required: 30 minutes

Materials/Preparation:
A copy of the book

What To Do:
1. Show the book cover and ask students to predict events and what the piece is about.
2. As you read the book, look at the organization of this story. Does it have a beginning that gets your attention and gives clues about what is coming?
3. How do the details add to the story? Can you recall them without looking at the pictures?
4. Do you see a pattern? Do the ants always have a reason to move on?
5. Does the end leave you and the ants in a good spot? What makes it good?

How Does This Activity Connect to the Trait of Organization?
- Provides a strong, clear model of sequential organization
- Shows how organization provides a skeleton for the ideas to develop

Organization Activity 10

Book: *Going Home* by Eve Bunting

Grades: Fourth through eighth

Time Required: 30–45 minutes

Materials/Preparation:
1. A copy of the book
2. 4" x 6" or larger cards to use for sequencing statements; make approximately seven sequencing cards using text from the book; include introduction and conclusion, as well as several parts from the body
3. Markers

What To Do:
1. Read the book aloud.
2. Ask students to sequence the cards.
3. Discuss the characteristics that help the students identify the introduction, the body, and the conclusion. (Elicit transition words, sequencing, patterns, and evidence of pacing.)
4. With students working in pairs, pick another book and see if the same characteristics are present in its organizational structure.
5. Have students make their own sequencing cards for their book and share them with the group.

How Does This Activity Connect to the Trait of Organization?
- Students are better prepared for properly revising the organizational parts of their writing if they can identify qualities of organization.
- Students practice key organizational strategies of sequencing, linking, transitions, and pacing.

Organization Activity 11

Book: *Sleeping Ugly* by Jane Yolen

Grades: Fourth on up

Time Required: One to two hours

Materials/Preparation:
1. A copy of the book
2. Pencils, pens, and paper

What To Do:
1. Read the book aloud.
2. Brainstorm a list of other fairy tales with students.
3. Pick one and examine the beginning, middle, and ending.
4. Have students change the middle and the ending of this other fairy tale.
5. Have them write the new version and illustrate it.

How Does This Activity Connect to the Trait of Organization?
- Authors have to organize their ideas so they make sense. Students practice organizing their own middles and endings of a fairy tale, e.g., *The Three Little Pigs, Cinderella, Jack and the Beanstalk*
- Learning to identify the different qualities of organization will give students welcome insight as they create their own original works

Organization Activity 12

Book: *Meanwhile, Back at the Ranch* by Trinka Hakes Noble

Grades: All

Time Required: 30 minutes

Materials/Preparation:
A copy of the book

What To Do:
1. Read the book aloud.
2. Discuss how one page is about low-key town and next page is about high-key ranch—the pattern includes alternating those two.
3. As a group, brainstorm other possible contrasts.
4. Have students work in pairs to make a class book using the close "Meanwhile, back at school, _____," and "Meanwhile, back at home," _____" on the other side.

How Does This Activity Connect to the Trait of Organization?
• Using a pattern to teach organization for putting a book together
• Showing a different way of organizing ideas

Organization Activity 13

Book: *The Old Man and His Door* by Gary Soto

Grades: Kindergarten through sixth

Time Required: 30–45 minutes

Materials/Preparation:
1. A copy of the book
2. Pencils, pens, and paper
3. Strips of paper for sentences from the book

What To Do:
1. Have students illustrate and write about (if appropriate) the order of events in the story. The number of pictures required could vary depending upon the skills of the students.
2. Select sentences from various parts of the text and record on strips of paper. Help students place these in the proper order.

How Does This Activity Connect to the Trait of Organization?
• Shows sequential organization and a sense of resolution

Voice

- Compare the voices of two different authors exploring the same topic or idea.

- After reading a variety of different picture books, make a list of all the words that can describe voice—angry, passionate, thoughtful, considerate, loving, mean-spirited, charming, eloquent, and so forth.

- Play "Hearing voices" by reading passages from familiar authors' works and matching their styles to their books.

- Make a list of places you notice voice making a difference—the type of books/print you like to read (what kind of voice is it?)—the things that you don't like to read (what kind of voice is it?).

- Pick a famous person and explain an important concept or idea to that person in picture book format.

- Write a letter to an author whose book(s) you love.

Voice Activity 1

Book: *What You Know First* by Patricia MacLachlan

Grades: All

Time Required: At least 45–60 minutes, but can be an extended writing project

Materials/Preparation:
1. A copy of the book
2. Pencils, pens, and paper

What To Do:
1. Discuss with students their earliest memories of where they were born, lived, and grew up. Allow them to imagine as far back as they can. Some will remember early childhood, others will not. It's OK—just help them roll back time to the moment they first recall.
2. Model what you mean by sharing a memory of your own. Include in your description people, places, sights, sounds, smells—even if they are very random.
3. As students talk, emphasize that all people have their own memories. No one will have the same even if they grew up in exactly the same places. Emphasize that the individual experience is what makes a good seedbed for an idea to write or draw.
4. As students talk more and more, encourage them to draw pictures of moments they remember, colors, shapes, places, dates—whatever. The more you talk as a group, the clearer their own memories will become. The more they capture in words or phrases, drawings, or impressions, the better.
5. Now read the book aloud. This should not take more than about 10 minutes, even if you do a dramatic reading with lots of pauses and thoughtful quiet time.
6. As you read, encourage students to add more to their pictures or words as they think of them.
7. After the reading, let students talk. Did they like this book? Did it make them feel anything? What did they feel? Record these comments so all students can see.
8. Ask them about their favorite parts. Reread those pages or parts of them. Why are those passages so memorable? (Word choice will be key here!)
9. When the discussion ends, ask students to look at their own words, phrases, or drawings. Do clear images of their early memories begin to emerge?
10. Have them write and draw more about these memories. They can use the same format as the book. Perhaps they, too, had to move when they were little and miss the place they first knew. Others may have another memory to share. Another place, time, and sense can be captured in words and/or pictures. Encourage students to decide for themselves if they have anything to share on this topic and to make an author's decision about the best way to share it. It may be a short scenario, or a longer piece.
11. Whatever students decide to do, let it be their decision. Show them how different students are approaching this topic in unique ways. Encourage this—and model it by writing or drawing a piece of the memory you shared earlier.

12. Display these early drafts. Encourage students to borrow ideas from each other. If you wish, ask students to refine their work by rethinking word choices, strong verbs, and clear imagery. Use both text and pictures to make these mental pictures come to life. Some students will want to go on with their work and take it to a polished, publishable stage. Others will be satisfied with their draft. Allow students to make those choices for themselves. Remember, this is a lesson on VOICE, so we want them to have time and opportunity to discover their own voices.

How Does This Activity Connect to the Trait of Voice?
- Validates individual experiences that are different from the experiences of others
- Rewards risk—making personal writer's decisions that may not be the same as their neighbor's
- Provides the opportunity to hear the voices of others
- Connects voice to word choice
- Allows voice to emerge over time, not assuming that it will "pop out" on the first try

Voice Activity 2

Book: *I Am the Dog, I Am the Cat* by Donald Hall

Grades: Second through fifth

Time Required: 45–60 minutes

Materials/Preparation:
1. A copy of the book
2. Multiple copies of typed sections of the book

What To Do:
1. Brainstorm characteristics of dogs and/or cats. Use pictures to help get ideas.
2. Read the book aloud in a "normal" voice.
3. Distribute sections of the story to pairs of students to come up with voices for the cat or dog.
4. Have students read their parts in a voice they think matches the animal and the message.
5. As a group, discuss their "voice choices" and which they found most effective.
6. Let students read the piece again and try out new voices.

How Does This Activity Connect to the Trait of Voice?
- Matching tone to text context, voice
- Listening to other voices and trying out new voices

Voice Activity 3

Book: *I Am the Dog, I Am the Cat* by Donald Hall

Grades: Fourth on up

Time Required: 30–45 minutes

Materials/Preparation:
1. A copy of the book
2. Pencils, pens, and paper

What To Do:
1. Read the book aloud.
2. How were the cat and the dog different? Brainstorm and chart in columns.
3. If we gave the dog the cat's attitude, what would we have to change?
4. Choose one moment from the book and change the dog's and cat's roles. Model for the class.
5. Discuss how the dog and the cat are each unique. Are your friends unique? Are you?
6. Pick two other different animals and list their traits (e.g., a bird and a fish). You may want to demonstrate using an apple and an orange.
7. Change or rewrite the story using two different animals or combine pairs of animals to make a class book.

How Does This Activity Connect to the Trait of Voice?
- Highlights differences and similarities between two things
- Emphasizes how differences define a personality
- Links individuality with voice

Voice Activity 4

Book: *I Am The Dog, I Am The Cat* by Donald Hall

Grades: All

Time Required: 30 minutes

Materials/Preparation:
1. A copy of the book
2. Pencils, pens, and paper

What To Do:
1. Have two students practice role playing the dog and the cat (even dressed up as the characters).
2. Read the book aloud.
3. Make two lists for students to see, one for the dog and one for the cat.
4. Ask: What is the dog's voice? What words are used to get the impression across? Then do the same thing for the cat.
5. Have students write about two animals/things that are opposites by focusing on different voices (cat and mouse, horse and cow, truck and car, girl and boy).

How Does This Activity Connect to the Trait of Voice?
- This is a good example of contrasting voices.
- Each subject needs to portray itself differently, and learn to use just the right words to express specific characteristics and voice of that animal or object.

Voice Activity 5

Book: *White Socks Only* by Evelyn Coleman

Grades: Intermediate

Time Required: 30 minutes

Materials/Preparation:
1. A copy of the book
2. Pencils, pens, and paper

What To Do:
1. Have students listen for words or sentences that capture the voices of the granddaughter in the first couple of pages and grandma when she is younger and throughout the story.
2. List the main characters.
3. Read the book aloud.
4. As you read, have students select one character and listen to the piece from that person's point of view.
5. Have students share their lists by character. Reread the book if needed to help expand the list.
6. Have the students write from one of the other character's point of view (Chicken Man, statue of the soldier, angry white man, old black woman, Mama, other black people, bystanders on the street or in the park) and add to the story.
7. Link this activity to the trait of voice and explain its criteria as students rewrite the story from a specific point of view.

How Does This Activity Connect to the Trait of Voice?
- Identifying the voices of the characters and their feelings gives the students a model
- By changing the point of view of the story and becoming another character, students practice writing in different voices

Voice Activity 6

Book: *Hoops* by Robert Burleigh

Grades: Intermediate on up

Time Required: 30–40 minutes

Materials/Preparation:
1. A copy of the book
2. Examples of Nike (or any easily recognized company) advertisements from magazines, newspapers, television, or radio (with permission to use)

What To Do:
1. Show the advertisements.
2. Have students list words that describe the voice or tone of the advertisement.
3. What is the message that is being sold? How is it created with words?
4. Read the book aloud.
5. Discuss the voice/tone of this book. What makes it intense? (Focus on words, sentence structure, and punctuation.) How is it similar to an advertisement?
6. Have students pick a sport and write an advertisement. Have the students focus on the voice/tone of the piece (intense, carefree, age-specific, etc.). Ask: What are you trying to sell?

How Does This Activity Connect to the Trait of Voice?
- The powerful messages of the advertisements are very much a part of today's society. Their tone and voice send more than just a message about sports equipment.
- *Hoops* is another example of the intensity words can have and the voice is expressed by carefully selected words.

Voice Activity 7

Books: *Antics!* by Catherine Hepworth
Two Bad Ants by Chris Van Allsburg

Grades: All

Time Required: One to two class periods

Materials/Preparation:
1. A copy of both books
2. Dictionary
3. Thesaurus or book of synonyms
4. Pencils, pens, and paper

What To Do:
1. Discuss with students a typical day in an ant's life.
2. Read *Antics!*
3. Have students list their own A–Z "ant" words using a dictionary.
4. Read *Two Bad Ants*. As you read the story, ask students to visualize the experience of these "naughty ants."
5. Using the ant's point of view, have students write about discovering a kitchen with heavenly morsels of food or a delightful picnic spot, incorporating as many "ant" words as they can.

How Does This Activity Connect to the Trait of Voice?
- Explores other points of view
- Establishes tone for students' own writing
- Identifies purpose and audience for writing

Voice Activity 8

Book: *Dear Children of the Earth* by Schim Schimmel

Grades: All

Time Required: 60 minutes

Materials/Preparation:
1. A copy of the book
2. Pencils, pens, and paper

What To Do:
1. Read the book aloud.
2. Choose one or more of the following activities:
   a) Who is doing the talking? Draw or write how Mother Earth feels.
   b) Have animals "write" back to Mother Earth.
   c) Have animals "write" to children.
   d) Children respond to Mother Earth with a plan. What can they do?

How Does This Activity Connect to the Trait of Voice?
- Practicing voice by assuming the role of an animal
- Looking at point of view through different eyes
- Writing informational pieces with voice appropriate to purpose and audience

Voice Activity 9

Book: *Fly Away Home* by Eve Bunting

Grades: Elementary on up

Time Required: Three 30-minute sessions

Materials/Preparation:
1. A copy of the book
2. Pencils, pens, and paper

What To Do:
1. Read the story aloud.
2. Discuss the topic of homelessness and how it might feel. Ask students why the characters don't want to be noticed.
3. Read it again and have students identify words that help them understand the feelings, such as in the boy's encounter with the bird. Ask how the author portrays the boy's feelings.

Suggested Activity:
Have each student write a sequel and share it with the class or group in which the boy and his father find a home. Or, have them write what happens next in this story. Does the boy get discovered? What happens?

How Does This Activity Connect to the Trait of Voice?
• Identifying voice by examining an author's style
• Exploring their own voices as they rewrite the ending

Voice Activity 10

Book: *The Snowman* by Raymond Briggs

Grades: Kindergarten through 12th

Time Required: 45–60 minutes

Materials/Preparation:
1. Copies of the book for small groups
2. Pencils, pens, and paper
3. Copies of the voice rubric appropriate to age
4. Optional: the video *The Snowman,* 26 minutes, ISBN 0-7912-0007-8

What To Do:
1. Group students by four or five and give each group a copy of the book.
2. Have the groups "read" the wordless picture book. At the end of each page, groups should stop and allow time for each student to record feelings on individual papers. (For young writers, let them capture the moods, feelings, and tones in pictures and allow time to explain their choices.)
3. After all groups have finished, have them share their feelings with the whole group. You should have many different responses since the piece changes its tone as it progresses.
4. Record these responses so students can see the varied voices that each reader "heard" from this piece. Group the responses by type: sad, lonely, happy, adventurous, and so forth.
5. Discuss the quality of voice using the rubric. Help students understand that writing can purposefully change its voice as it develops, but there must be a strong sense of reader-writer interaction throughout; otherwise, the reader loses interest and doesn't want to finish the piece. Ask them how their descriptions of voice might change if the story itself changed. What if it got scary, suspenseful, or silly?
6. If you wish, show the video. Ask if students identify more voice descriptors with music added.
7. Have students talk about other books with a lot of voice. If possible, go to the library and find examples, or look through books in your classroom. As they find strong examples, have them record descriptors of the type of voice in their writer's notebooks or on a bulletin board where examples are collected and displayed.

Additional Activity:
When students find other picture books with a lot of voice, have them match music pieces to the text. Part of what makes the video of *The Snowman* so effective is the music. See if students can create similar matches of music to voice for their own books.

How Does This Activity Connect to the Trait of Voice?
- Reading a piece with a focus on identifying the voice
- Connecting music to voice
- Describing voice with specific vocabulary
- Using the rubric that describes the quality of voice to find other examples

Use Picture Books To Teach the Trait of

Word Choice

- Make a list of striking phrases or words you find in picture books.

- Highlight active verbs.

- Examine the proportion of types of words found in picture books: How many verbs? How many nouns? How many adjectives and adverbs?

- Discuss the different word choice techniques picture book authors use to create pictures in the mind.

- Write a picture book using colorless, redundant words. Now rewrite it using colorful, illustrative language. Compare and contrast.

- Find examples of "everyday" words used well.

Word Choice Activity 1

Book: *Earth: The Elements* by Ken Robbins

Grades: Elementary on up

Time Required: At least 45 minutes

Materials/Preparation:
1. A copy of the book
2. Materials from encyclopedias, textbooks, and other physical science reference materials on the same topics as the book: volcanoes; earthquakes; mountains; igneous, sedimentary, and metamorphic rock; fossils; and so on
3. A place to display words and phrases that students discover—chart pack, big piece of butcher paper, chalk-/whiteboard

What To Do:
1. Have students help collect written and visual material about the topics in the book. Have them consult textbooks, encyclopedias, the Internet, magazines, and any other resource readily available. The important thing is to have a variety.
2. Assign teams to read and discuss the material on their assigned topics.
3. After having students sort the material, ask them to record the vocabulary writers use to describe the topic. Do they use scientific language? Do they use simple words? Do they use a combination? What about the verbs? Are they passive or active? Write their observations somewhere other students can see and respond.
4. Discuss the different ways authors used language in different pieces about the same topic, and have students rank the pieces by which they found most interesting. See if they explain verbally or in writing. Then have them rank and sort the pieces by which they think had the best information and explain why. Now have them sort the pieces by who they think the intended audience is. Students? What ages? Adults? Scientists? The general public?
5. Discuss each ranking and sorting activity. Do all the groups come to the same conclusions? Why or why not? Have them make group decisions about how a writer should choose words to fit the purpose and audience of their writing. Would you always use the same vocabulary? Why or why not?
6. Have groups pull out favorite descriptive phrases or words in their pieces—ones that linger in their minds, or clarify a difficult concept that was both interesting and understandable. See how many come from which sources. Ask them where they find examples of expository writing that they enjoy most.
7. If time allows, ask students to consider using visuals—pictures, charts, graphs, and so forth, to enhance the meaning of the text. Which trait is this? Or is there one … yet?

How Does This Activity Connect to the Trait of Word Choice?
- Explores the use of specific, content-centered vocabulary
- Compares and contrasts language use for different purposes and audiences
- Develops an eye for key words or phrases that work particularly well
- Demonstrates that it's OK to make even very technical writing interesting to read

Word Choice Activity 2

Book: *Wilfrid Gordon McDonald Partridge* by Mem Fox

Grades: Third through 10th

Time Required: Two to three class periods

Materials/Preparation:
1. A copy of the book
2. Pencils, pens, and paper

What To Do:
1. Read the book aloud.
2. In groups, have students brainstorm about memories.
3. Have students write individual lists of their memories using the following prompt: You are 75 years old and are assembling in a basket your favorite childhood memories to share. Describe what you would put in the basket, the story behind each object, and with whom you would share your memory basket.
4. Share favorites with the class.

How Does This Activity Connect to the Trait of Word Choice?
- Encourages students to use energetic verbs, vivid words, and phrases
- Focuses students on the specifics and details of the objects that help them focus their writing and use descriptive words

Word Choice Activity 3

Book: *Wilfrid Gordon McDonald Partridge* by Mem Fox

Grades: Third through sixth

Time Required: 60 minutes

Materials/Preparation:
1. A copy of the book
2. Pencils, pens, and paper

What To Do:
1. Explain what a simile is and write examples for students to see.
2. Have students help you substitute words.
3. Read the book aloud. Have students raise their hands when they hear a simile and identify it.
   Example: voice like a giant, as precious as gold
4. Have students write about a memory they want to share and include at least one simile.
   Tip: They may have to play with the way they use the words to clarify the simile.
   Example: She had eyes like bowling balls (big and round).

How Does This Activity Connect to the Trait of Word Choice?
- Works with words to create images
- Chooses words with precision for maximum effect

Word Choice Activity 4

Book: *My Mama Had a Dancing Heart* by Libba Moore Gray

Grades: Second through fourth (with help from an older class to create partners)

Time Required: 45 minutes

Materials/Preparation:
1. A copy of the book
2. Pencils, pens, and paper

What To Do:
1. Read the book aloud.
2. Have students write down phrases that appeal to them. With younger students, use the buddy system: The younger student can tell the "buddy" (older) student when they hear a phrase they like, and the older student writes it down.
3. Have students illustrate their favorite phrases.
4. Talk about how these words create pictures in their minds.
5. Connect their illustrations to the text in the book (buddies can help), and then display all the illustrations with text.

How Does This Activity Connect to the Trait of Word Choice?
- Students listen for language use and think about how they can illustrate these word images.
- Students learn how to choose precise words to create feelings and emotions.

Word Choice Activity 5

Book: *My Mama Had a Dancing Heart* by Libba Moore Gray

Grades: All

Time Required: 60 minutes

Materials/Preparation:
1. A copy of the book
2. Music to represent the seasons (Vivaldi's *Four Seasons,* George Winston's *Fall, Spring,* and so forth, the *Nutcracker, The Grand Canyon Suite)*

What To Do:
1. Read the story aloud and show the pictures.
2. Read again, and have students listen for language and phrases.
3. Discuss descriptive phrases for each season.
4. Divide students into four groups—one for each season.
5. Have groups work with music to dance/dramatize sessions.

How Does This Activity Connect to the Trait of Word Choice?
* Students understand word rhythms
* Students select words to create vivid imagery

Word Choice Activity 6

Books: *Earthdance* by Joanne Ryder
Papa, Please Get the Moon for Me by Eric Carle

Grades: First through third

Time Required: Two to three class periods

Materials/Preparation:
1. A copy of both books
2. Chart paper
3. Markers

What To Do:
1. Read *Earthdance* aloud.
2. Discuss the illustrative language, and list words or phrases on chart paper.
3. Discuss the "pictures" these words create.
4. Discuss moon rotation and its phases.
5. Read *Papa, Please Get the Moon for Me* aloud.
6. List words and phrases that could be used to create connections to the moon.
7. Write a story entitled "Moon Dance" using the words and illustrations of the students.
8. Have some students create and tape music that makes the moon dance.
9. Have students read "Moon Dance" with their music playing in the background.

How Does This Activity Connect to the Trait of Word Choice?
- Students learn to use "colorful" words to communicate a thought or picture for others
- Students connect words to images and feelings

Word Choice Activity 7

Book: *The Old Man and His Door* by Gary Soto

Grades: Kindergarten through sixth

Time Required: 30–45 minutes

Materials/Preparation:
1. A copy of the book
2. Pencils, pens, and paper

What To Do:
1. As a group, reread the story and list the descriptive vocabulary (e.g., "mountains of suds"). Allow students to select and illustrate one.
2. Encourage students to brainstorm the meaning of new words.

How Does This Activity Connect to the Trait of Word Choice?
- Illustrates how using a word incorrectly can completely change a story's meaning

Word Choice Activity 8

Book: *Hoops* by Robert Burleigh

Grades: Fourth through sixth

Time Required: 30–45 minutes

Materials/Preparation:
1. A copy of the book
2. Pencils, pens, and paper

What To Do:
1. Read the book aloud.
2. In small groups, have students condense each page, in order, to a single word that expresses the skill or emotion revealed. Have them write the words vertically to create a poem that parallels *Hoops.*
3. Have students think of a different sport they love. Have them describe it using alliteration.
4. Have them pack the energy of one moment into an illustration of that sport.
5. Have students expand this into a longer descriptive piece. Will adding information take anything away from the intensity, or can it add to it?

How Does This Activity Connect to the Trait of Word Choice?
- Students listen to the singing of the words used in alliteration and to how they "propel" the reader through the game, giving it vitality.
- Students practice condensing words and phrases as they examine their precision in text.

Word Choice Activity 9

Book: *Hoops* by Robert Burleigh

Grades: Intermediate

Time Required: 30–40 minutes

Materials/Preparation:
1. A copy of the book
2. A few selected sentences or phrases from the book
3. Something to hide the cover of the book
4. Pencils, pens, and paper

What To Do:
1. Hand out a sentence or phrase to a small group of students.
2. Have students discuss the imagery and word choice. What does the sentence refer to or describe?
3. Have students share ideas and get other interpretations.
4. Have students rewrite the sentences by replacing words in the sentence with synonyms or antonyms. Discuss how the imagery and tone change.
5. Read the book aloud. HIDE the cover and DON'T READ THE FIRST PAGE. ("Hoops. The Game. Feel it.")
6. Ask: What is the story about? Discuss how the words help create the image of basketball.
7. Have students summarize the book and write their own first line. Then compare it to the original.

How Does This Activity Connect to the Trait of Word Choice?
- Students see firsthand that one word or phrase can create a mood or feeling or destroy it.
- The choice of words helps create very powerful and specific imagery. This book is an excellent model of word choice. The words are specific, intentional, and powerful. They work together like pieces in a puzzle, fitting together to describe one topic.

Word Choice Activity 10

Book: *I Love You the Purplest* by Barbara M. Joosse

Grades: All

Time Required: Two 30-minute sessions

Materials/Preparation:
1. A copy of the book
2. Examples of colors (paper, paint, ink)
3. Pictures with strong, deep colors

What To Do:
1. Read the book aloud.
2. Talk about and identify examples of word choice. Ask: What lines do you remember? Reread sections of the book if needed to trigger students' memories.
3. Reread the description of why the mother loves her two sons. "I love you the bluest!" and "I love you the reddest!"
4. Discuss the choice of words and the images they bring to mind.
5. Have students pick a color and write about the qualities and objects that color brings to mind.
6. Have students think of someone they are close to and describe that person using a color. Use the author's examples as a model.

Additional Activity:
Have students write a list of colors and what they could be related to, e.g., green = envy, white = purity, and so forth (May require some research.)

How Does This Activity Connect to the Trait of Word Choice?
• Students explore working on word choice to create an example based on the model.
• Students use specific choices of words and objects to express what's special about the person they are writing about.

Word Choice Activity 11

Book: *Verdi* by Janell Cannon

Grades: All

Time Required: Two 30-minute sessions

Materials/Preparation:
1. A copy of the book
2. Resource materials on other animals
3. Copies of a couple of pages from the book with all the descriptive, lively words/verbs deleted and replaced with a blank line
4. Thesaurus
5. Pencils, pens, and paper

What To Do:
1. Have students make predictions about the story based on the cover.
2. List the ideas, descriptions, and personality traits of the snake, Verdi, based on the predictions.
3. Read the book aloud.
4. Make a new list of descriptions, personality traits, and so forth.
5. Compare the two lists. What is the same? What is different?
6. Hand out the prepared pages.
7. Assign groups of students to certain characteristics of Verdi. For example: He can be shy, ferocious, intimidated, sad, curious, and so forth.
8. Have students fill in the blanks with different lively words using a thesaurus or other resource based on the personality trait they are trying to represent.
9. Have students read their rewritten pages to the class.

Additional Activity:
Write a similar story about an animal that changes its color or appearance (e.g., ugly duckling into a swan, caterpillar into a butterfly).

How Does This Activity Connect to the Trait of Word Choice?
- Students find descriptive, lively words to create a desired tone.
- Students are creative as they write their own pieces.

Word Choice Activity 12

Book: *Have You Seen Trees?* by Joanne Oppenheim

Grades: All

Time Required: Two 30-minute sessions

Materials/Preparation:
1. A copy of the book
2. Pictures of trees
3. A place to take a walk and look at trees
4. Resources for different types of trees (pamphlets, encyclopedia articles, books, Internet reference sites, etc.)

What To Do:
1. Read the book aloud.
2. If possible, have students take a walk and look at some trees, or look at pictures of trees.
3. Have students list descriptive words or phrases that describe the trees—similarities and differences.
4. Have students write a description about a tree for each season of the year or for a variety of tree types.
5. Have students read their descriptions aloud without revealing tree names. Can they guess based on the descriptions? Be sure that students are not making their guesses based on pictures!

How Does This Activity Connect to the Trait of Word Choice?
- Students identify and write specific words to describe a particular type of tree, which develops precision in word choice.
- Students practice using precise nouns and modifiers.

Word Choice Activity 13

Book: *My Grandma Lived in Gooligulch* by Graeme Base

Grades: Fifth through eighth

Time Required: 30 minutes

Materials/Preparation:
1. A copy of the book
2. Dictionary
3. World map

What To Do:
1. Discuss the six traits.
2. Read the book aloud.
3. Discuss language differences.
4. Show map and locate Australia.
5. Create a word bank with the unfamiliar words and add to the list as the year progresses.
6. Identify meanings in the book using context clues.
7. Rewrite the book in American English; discuss the differences—there are many ways to say the same thing!

How Does This Activity Connect to the Trait of Word Choice?
• Focuses students on vocabulary differences
• Develops using context clues to learn new words

Word Choice Activity 14

Book: *Amber on the Mountain* by Tony Johnston

Grades: Elementary/middle school

Time Required: 45 minutes

Materials/Preparation:
1. A copy of the book
2. Pencils, pens, and paper

What To Do:
1. Read the book aloud.
2. Reread pages with simile and metaphor examples.
3. Brainstorm "powerful" words/phrases using ideas found in the story with students.
4. Define and discuss similes and metaphors.
5. Reread some lines without simile or metaphors: "Her tongue curled to her upper lip in concentration …" (like a lizard stalking a bug).
6. Discuss why and how similes and metaphors make the words and story more interesting.
7. Have students write and/or illustrate similes and metaphors from this book or other books.

How Does This Activity Connect to the Trait of Word Choice?
- Similes and metaphors are powerful tools for students to understand the trait
- Students' expand their choice of words to be more precise

Word Choice Activity 15

Book: *Double Trouble in Walla Walla* by Andrew Clements

Grades: Third through 12th

Time Required: 45 minutes

Materials/Preparation:
1. A copy of the book
2. A place to display results of brainstorming activity
3. Pencils, pens, and paper

What To Do:
1. Have students name all the word pairs they can think of, such as: double trouble, jingle jangle, hodge podge, and so forth. Display the list and leave room to add more.
2. As you read the book aloud, have students write down any word pairs in the story that they liked that aren't already on the list.
3. Discuss the story and its conclusion. Have pairs of students write a new ending to the story that takes it in a different direction. Or, have them write a whole new story, beginning to end, using as many word pairs from the list or their imagination as they can. If a holiday is approaching, they may want to write twists and turns on popular holiday stories.
4. Give them plenty of time to write, revise, and share their work with other groups. See which group was able to work in the most wacky word pairs. Remember—they have to make sense in the context of the story.
5. Have students illustrate a few of their pages.
6. Have all the pages laminated and comb bound into a book.
7. Arrange for students to read their books to a class of younger students, and have the younger ones talk about word choice before the older students come for a visit. Group younger and older students together and rotate the stories.
8. Have younger students write wacky word pair thank-you notes to the class of older students after the visit. (This could be the beginning of a very positive and productive relationship between the two classes that can be nurtured and encouraged all year long!)
9. Leave the wacky word pair books in the library or media center for everyone to enjoy!

How Does This Activity Connect to the Trait of Word Choice?
- Playing with words creates wacky pairs that rhyme
- Listening to the sounds of the words and their syllabication helps choose good pairs of words and those that fit best in the sentences
- Practicing precision with words is fun

Sentence Fluency

- Read poetry aloud and ask, "What makes the language flow?" Make a list of ideas. Do the same with prose selections.

- Use choral reading to practice hearing where and how sentences and phrases begin and end. Emphasize inflections, pauses, and so forth.

- Type the text of a picture book without any sentence breaks; then rewrite it, showing the natural fluency through sentences, patterns, and punctuation.

- List sentence beginnings to see how much variety authors use.

- Read two or three picture books and count how many simple, compound, and complex sentences are in each. Why do some sentence patterns work better in certain sections of the text?

- Tell a story/explain a concept aloud before you try to write it. Ask a partner to write down the beginning of each sentence as you speak.

Sentence Fluency Activity 1

Book: *The Ghost Dance* by Alice McLerran

Grades: All (but especially middle level and high school)

Time Required: Several class periods (about two hours total)

Materials/Preparation:
1. A copy of the book
2. Typed cards with selected sections of the text for small groups to read

What To Do:
1. Read the book aloud, along with the author and illustrator notes at the end that tell the history of the Paiute Indian Ghost Dance. See if students can connect the themes of integrity, non-violence, and social and environmental health to other great world philosophies and traditions.
2. Discuss students' impressions of the story and pictures.
3. Read the book again. Have students jot down any key words or phrases they like as they listen.
4. Have students share their key words or phrases. Discuss what makes something pleasing to the ear. Is it rhythm? Is it cadence? What is fluency, anyway?
5. Divide the class into groups. Pass out typed cards. Have students examine them carefully. How do the sentences begin? Is there good variety in sentence patterns? What about length? Is this piece fluent?
6. Do a choral reading of the book. There are many ways to do this. One suggestion: Sequence the groups so as one finishes reading, the other begins until the text is complete.
7. Allow students time to rehearse their parts, emphasizing that they can read whole passages together, separate words by single voices, or chime in together for emphasis. Since each group has a small amount of text, have them read FLUENTLY, and consider how to make it sound pleasing to the ear.
8. Perform the choral reading as a class. Let students make changes, rehearse more, and then do it again. They may wish to add music, sound effects, or their own visuals. Choral readings are deceptively difficult, so allow plenty of time. If they do well, have them perform for other students, parents, or staff.
9. To debrief, refer students to the sentence fluency writing criteria. Have them identify the descriptors for strong performance they considered as they did the choral reading. Have them select other texts for choral readings as well. This lesson can be repeated with many variations. Fluency is a very oral trait, so the more students learn to hear the language, the better.

How Does This Activity Connect to the Trait of Sentence Fluency?
- Hearing beautiful language used well to develop an ear for fluency
- Examining sentences, phrases, and individual words as they connect
- Using speaking skills to emphasize rhythm and flow
- Discussing techniques that writers use to make their work sound good

Sentence Fluency Activity 2

Book: *All the Places To Love* by Patricia MacLachlan

Grades: Third through sixth

Time Required: One to two class periods

Materials/Preparation:
1. A copy of the book
2. Pencils, pens, and paper

What To Do:
1. Read the book aloud.
2. Select one of the following activities:
   a) Have students write a poem using some of the phrases in the book.
   b) Rewrite as reader's theater. Cast students in roles of Eli, momma, papa, grandfather, and grandmother. Pair remaining students or form small groups to read shorter descriptive passages on each page.
   c) Have students draw pictures they see in their minds, adding phrases they like from the book.
   d) Have students write a poem about a favorite place.

How Does This Activity Connect to the Trait of Sentence Fluency?
- Students learn to listen to the phrasing of the piece.
- Students identify key phrases and words they especially like.
- Students hear the language spoken as they share their reader's theater versions.

Sentence Fluency Activity 3

Book: *A Drop of Water: A Book of Science and Wonder* by Walter Wick

Grades: All

Time Required: 30–60 minutes

Materials/Preparation:
1. A copy of the book
2. Pencils, pens, and paper

What To Do:
1. Read an example of a process from the book.
2. Discuss and write down how the author uses a variety of sentence types to describe each process.
3. Read another example and have students listen for sentence fluency.
4. Have the students rewrite a paragraph without using sentence fluency, making it as boring as possible (e.g., short sentences all beginning the same way or one long, run-on sentence).
5. Have students share their paragraphs. Compare them with the original piece.
6. Have students describe a process in writing, e.g., making a peanut butter and jelly sandwich or tying shoes. (Science concepts studied in class are also excellent topics. This would help with integration of curriculum.) Have them focus on sentence fluency using the author's examples.

How Does This Activity Connect to the Trait of Sentence Fluency?
- Nonfiction, factual writing does not have to be boring, but can be interesting and concise
- Looking for different sentence patterns helps with revising pieces for fluency

Sentence Fluency Activity 4

Book: *Have You Seen Trees?* by Joanne Oppenheim

Grades: Third on up

Time Required: 30–45 minutes

Materials/Preparation:
1. A copy of the book
2. Pencils, pens, and paper; art supplies
3. Sentence fluency rubric for each student

What To Do:
1. Discuss students' favorite trees. Have students select a favorite tree from the ones mentioned.
2. Read the book aloud, having students pay attention to long and stretchy, short and snappy sentence fluency.
3. Have students write a short paragraph about their tree while referring to the sentence fluency rubric.
4. Have students share their writing.
5. Have students illustrate their writing.
6. Compile a book of their writings and illustrations, organized by season or the way they described the trees.

How Does This Activity Connect to the Trait of Sentence Fluency?
- Students hear good literature.
- Students practice using voice to personalize, flavor, and develop their own style.
- Students listen to the rhythm of written language.
- Students practice using the sentence fluency trait based on the model.

Conventions

- Look at picture books with an editor's eye. Can you find any mistakes?

- Select several picture books that contain dialogue: What convention rules do they follow?

- Make a list of the conventions that should be standard and another list of those things that the author should personally control.

- Deliberately make five spelling, five punctuation, five capitalization, and five grammar/usage errors in your own picture book text. Ask someone to find and correct them. (They can correct other things they find, too!)

- Type your picture book onto the computer and use the spell checker, grammar checker, and thesaurus options. What do you have to know about conventions to make the best use of these tools?

In general, the trait of conventions is not one that lends itself well to being taught through picture books. You can use them as wonderful examples, however, of how conventions make the text more readable when done well.

Conventions Activity 1

Book: *Yo! Yes?* by Chris Raschka

Grades: All (but especially for early writers)

Time Required: 30–45 minutes minimum

Materials/Preparation:
1. A copy of the book
2. Pencils, pens, and paper

What To Do:
1. Have students record the text below as you read it to them. They can also do this by themselves, and you'll get better results if they work in pairs or small groups.

   Yo Yes Hey
   Who You Me
   Yes you Oh
   What's up Not much
   Why No fun
   … and so on

   To make this more challenging for older students, have them write the words in order without any line changes. The way the text is written here is just like in the book (one line per page), which helps the reader understand the story.
2. Have students add punctuation to make the story flow and have meaning.
3. Compare the different groups' changes to the punctuation to see if the meanings change.
4. Show students the book and its punctuation that helps the reader understand. Does it resemble any of the students' writing? Are the student versions different due to changes in punctuation?
5. Have students perform their stories.
6. Discuss the use and abuse of editing.

How Does This Activity Connect to the Trait of Conventions?
- Students use a variety of punctuation to make meaning clear.
- Editing is an important part of the writing process.
- Students do their own editing.
- Students think about editing and conventions in a new way.

Conventions Activity 2

Book: *The Day I Swapped My Dad for Two Goldfish* by Neil Gaiman

Grades: Intermediate

Time Required: 30 minutes

Materials/Preparation:
1. Several pages of the book on transparencies or shown on opaque projector
2. Several other books with dialogue
3. Examples of cartoon dialogue bubbles (cartoons from the newspaper are a good source)
4. Pencils, pens, and paper
5. Page of dialogue with no punctuation for each student

What To Do:
1. Show examples of cartoon dialogue bubbles. Discuss why they are used.
2. Display pages of the book as you read it aloud.
3. Discuss the way the author chooses which words are in the bubble and which are not.
4. Have students pick dialogue from a book of their choice and write the dialogue (or a section of dialogue) using the cartoon bubbles that are modeled in the book, putting the dialogue in the bubbles.
5. Give students pages of dialogue with no punctuation. Have them fill in the punctuation by rewriting it in dialogue bubbles.

How Does This Activity Connect to the Trait of Conventions?
- Separating dialogue into cartoon bubbles shows students how to demonstrate conversation in writing.
- Experimenting with dialogue and ways to indicate changes in speaker leads to conventional use of punctuation.

Presentation

- Look at picture books with different styles of illustration and layout. Make a list of differences and commonalities.

- Cover up the words in a book and see if it is possible to follow the storyline without words.

- Have students tell a story using just the pictures as cues.

- Talk about how informational texts incorporate and use graphs and charts to enhance interest of the reader.

- Have students make lists of their favorite picture books. Look for similarities in presentation style.

- Look for books with unusual presentation style (such as *Amelia's Notebook* by Marissa Moss). What is it about the style of the book that makes it successful?

Presentation Activity 1

Books: *Amelia's Notebook* by Marissa Moss
The Polar Express by Chris Van Allsburg
Earth: The Elements by Ken Robbins

Grades: Fourth through 10th

Time required: Two 30-minute sessions

Materials/Preparation:
1. A copy of each book
2. Pencils, pens, and paper

What To Do:
1. Show students the three books.
2. Discuss the style of each and what tone the author was trying to achieve with the presentation.
3. Have students say which style they thought was most effective.
4. Have students choose the style that appealed to them the most and write and/or draw one page for the book using the same style.
5. Display pages. Have students suggest which author each picture best represents.

How Does This Activity Connect to the Trait of Presentation?
- Different styles of presentation are most effective with particular types of book.
- Presentation can reflect and enhance the author's voice.

Presentation Activity 2

Book: *Dear Diary* by Sarah Fanelli

Grades: Third through eighth

Time required: 45–60 minutes

Materials/Preparation:
1. A copy of the book
2. Old magazines
3. Pencils, pens, and paper

What To Do:
1. Read the book aloud and show it to students.
2. Discuss the style of presentation and the author's purpose in using it.
3. Have students create a diary page for themselves in a similar style, using cut-out images from magazines.

How Does This Activity Connect to the Trait of Presentation?
- Students connect the author's purpose with the presentation style
- Students learn how to use presentation to increase the impact of their ideas

References

Benedict, Susan, & Carlisle, Lenore. (Eds.). (1992). *Beyond words: Picture books for older readers and writers.* Portsmouth, NH: Heinemann. Paperback: ISBN 0-435-08710-X.

> A must-read resource for ideas on using picture books to enrich the lives of students from first grade through high school. Very practical suggestions and unit designs. Sprinkled with words of wisdom from such authors as Maurice Sendak, Dr. Seuss, David Macaulay, and Chris Van Allsburg, this readable reference book clearly points the way to using picture books with older readers and writers.

Fox, Mem. (1992). *Dear Mem Fox, I have read all your books even the pathetic ones; and other incidents in the life of a children's book author.* San Diego, CA: Harcourt Brace Jovanovich. Paperback: ISBN 0-15-658676-2.

> Do you love a good story? Mem Fox tells all in her wonderful autobiography, which deals primarily with her life as she becomes a children's picture book author. Her wit and wisdom are guaranteed to keep you reading. Powerful messages for writers, teachers, textbook publishers, and all readers of her stories.

Hall, Susan. (1990, 1994). *Using picture storybooks to teach literary devices: Recommended books for children and young adults* (Vols. 1–2). Phoenix, AZ: Oryx Press. Paperback: ISBN 0-89-774849-2.

> This annotated bibliography of picture books illustrates different literary devices. Arranged alphabetically by topic—allusion, flashback, foreshadowing, imagery, personification, poetic justice, and so on—with picture book titles and suggestions for developing a better understanding of each literary device. A very helpful shortcut to collecting books on special topics or for literature units focusing on special skills.

Lu, Ji. (2000). *The art of writing: Lu Chi's wen fu* (Rev. ed., Sam Hamill, Trans.). Minneapolis, MN: Milkweed Editions. Paperback: ISBN 157-131-4121.

> As with all things done brilliantly, experts make it look easy. The practice and the pain of working through ineptness are rarely visible. Just so with writing. In fact, it's said that sportswriter Red Smith once said: Writing is easy. All you do is sit down at a typewriter and open a vein. The hard part of writing crosses cultures and centuries. The Wen Fu, written in 200 C.E., is reputed to be a spot-on description of the process, echoing so much of what writers do and feel in our contemporary cultures.

Author Index

Title Index

Teacher's note: While many picture books are suitable for both elementary and secondary students, we have added the YA code to those titles that would be of particular interest to young adults in grades 6–12.

More Great 6+1 Trait® Writing Products
From the Northwest Regional Educational Laboratory

Visit NWREL's entire collection of research-based publications at www.nwrel.org/comm/catalog/

Picture Books

Item #E013
Member $16.75 + shipping / **Nonmember $18.45** + shipping

Seeing With New Eyes

For primary students, writing can take many forms: drawings, scribbles, recordings, and text that goes every which way. The challenge for teachers is to see experimentation and playfulness of young writers not as errors, but as ways of learning. The sixth edition of *Seeing With New Eyes* is designed to do just that.

This 6+1 Trait® Writing guidebook helps teachers use the traits of good writing as a framework for instruction and scoring of prewriters as well as competent ones. While the main audience for the publication is teachers of kindergarten through second-grade students, the model can also be used effectively for older youngsters in special education and Limited English Proficiency classes.

Among the changes to the sixth edition are new scoring guides geared to giving effective feedback on a wide range of student work samples. Using the traits helps teachers focus their instruction, identifying the specific characteristics that contribute to good writing. (2005, 6th ed.; 317 pp.)

Item #E028
Member $23.40 + shipping / **Nonmember $26.45** + shipping

6+1 Trait® Writing: A Model That Works Video Set

Used in hundreds of classrooms throughout the country, the 6+1 TRAIT Writing assessment model works with current curriculum so teachers can accurately assess student writing growth, provide specific, meaningful feedback on student writing, and make appropriate decisions on lesson planning and instructional design.

This comprehensive video set provides tools and instruction to implement the 6+1 TRAIT Writing model in grades 2 through 12 and beyond. This professional, 8-tape set includes an introduction to the powerful 6+1 TRAIT model, 7 trait-specific videotapes, and a *Facilitator's Guide*. Each 8-minute, trait-specific video:
- Clearly defines one trait
- Summarizes the characteristics of the traits
- Describes how good use of the trait looks
- Explains scoring criteria illustrated with examples of actual student writing
- Provides practice scoring opportunities
- Offers insights from teachers using the model

The *Facilitator's Guide* reinforces and supplements the video series with scoring guides, samples of scored student writing, and instructions on how to optimize use of the videos. (2003; 144 pp.)

Item #E300
Member $399.60 + $12.99 shipping
Nonmember $424.00 + $12.99 shipping

Wee Can Write

The newest member of NWREL's 6+1 Trait® Writing family of resources, *Wee Can Write™* has evidently filled a niche. Written for teachers by teachers, this best-selling publication has only been out a short time, but has already been widely embraced by teachers of beginning writers across the country. Authors Carolyn McMahon and Peggy Warrick—with a combined 33 years in the elementary-level classroom—wrote the book having recognized the need for practical, easy-to-use instructional strategies to introduce the traits writing model to their youngest writers.

The 135-page teacher guide is organized around 36 renowned and readily available picture books, thematically categorized by the four seasons of the year. For each book title, activities are provided for the six traits of writing—skills that form the basis of effective writing at all ages and grade levels. These flexible lessons support an integrative approach to reading, writing, speaking, and creative artwork. Text is color-coded making it easy to distinguish information for the teacher versus instruction to be delivered to the students. (2005; 135 pp.)

Item #E009
Member $22.65 + shipping / **Nonmember $25.70** + shipping

6+1 Trait® Writing Rubric to Grade Converter

Teachers love a lot of things about the 6+1 TRAIT model: It helps them improve their writing instruction; it shows students what good writing looks like; and it creates a common vocabulary to discuss writing. But, the main drawback to the model has always been the time-consuming calculations required to convert rubric scores to grades.

NWREL offers a time-saving solution that ensures accuracy using reliable slide-chart technology. The Rubric to Grade Converter has the flexibility to work with the model's four-, five-, and six- point scales and can be used to grade writing on just one or up to all seven traits. (2005; 4 by 9 inches)

Item #E112
Member $9.75 + shipping / **Nonmember $10.60** + shipping

6+1 Trait® Writing Magnets

Ensure student comprehension of the 6+1 TRAIT Writing model with these colorful teaching aids. Designed to magnetically adhere to dry erase–type marker boards, each trait is featured on its own 7½ by 11-inch magnet with an icon that visually represents the trait's function. The magnets' large size means even students in the back of the classroom can clearly see and understand each trait. Teachers can use these magnets as a lecture/ teaching aid to introduce and reinforce the purpose of each trait and how it contributes to good writing. (2005; 7½ by 11 inches each)

Item #E110
Member $21.10 + shipping / **Nonmember $23.35** + shipping

ORDER FORM

1 HOW WILL YOU ORDER?

The fastest and easiest way to order is online at **www.nwrel.org/comm/catalog/**

By fax or phone (for credit card and purchase orders): fax 503-275-0458, phone 888-827-7241

By mail (for credit card, purchase order, check, or cash orders): NWREL Marketing Office, 101 S.W. Main Street, Ste. 500, Portland, OR 97204-3213

ALL SALES ARE FINAL AND RETURNS CANNOT BE ACCEPTED. REVIEW COPIES CANNOT BE PROVIDED.

2 HOW CAN WE CONTACT YOU?

Shipping Address: (please print or type)

Billing Address: (if different than shipping address; *credit card orders must be accompanied by the cardholder's mailing address*)

Name

Institution

Street address

City, state, ZIP

Daytime phone number ( )   E-mail address

3 WHAT ITEM(S) ARE YOU ORDERING?

Item #	Title	Quantity	Price	Subtotal

To receive the member discount, items must be shipped to an address in Oregon, Washington, Montana, Idaho, or Alaska.

Subtotal ordered $ _____

Postage and shipping (see below) $ _____

Total $ _____

4 HOW MUCH IS POSTAGE AND SHIPPING?

- Special shipping rates apply to the 6+1 Trait® Writing Toolbox and 6+1 Trait® Writing Video Set
- Orders are processed and shipped within 7 days.
- Orders shipped to locations in the United States where UPS delivery is not available will be shipped via first-class U.S. mail at the UPS ground rate.
- Orders shipped outside the United States, its possessions, and Canada are shipped via international air mail and require an additional 25% shipping charge.

Merchandise Subtotal	UPS Ground (10–14 days)	Third-Day UPS Air	Second-Day UPS Air
Less than $19.99	$ 4.50	$ 9.95	$17.45
$20.00–29.99	$ 6.50	$10.95	$18.45
$30.00–39.99	$ 8.50	$13.95	$21.45
$40.00–69.99	$11.50	$16.95	$24.45
$70.00–99.99	$15.50	$20.95	$28.45
$100.00–199.99	$19.50	$24.95	$32.45
$200.00 or more	10% of total	15% of total	20% of total

5 HOW ARE YOU PAYING?

☐ Purchase order from U.S. institution   ☐ Prepayment in U.S. dollars/check enclosed   ☐ VISA/MasterCard credit card (circle one)

PO #_____ (copy of purchase order must be enclosed)

Credit card number _____   Expiration date _____

Printed name on card _____   Signature _____